# From Basketball to the Beatles

# From Basketball to the Beatles

## In Search of Compelling Early Childhood Curriculum

**BEN MARDELL**

*Foreword by Eleanor Duckworth*

**HEINEMANN**
*Portsmouth, NH*

**Heinemann**
A division of Reed Elsevier Inc.
361 Hanover Street
Portsmouth, NH 03801–3912
www.heinemann.com

*Offices and agents throughout the world*

**Library of Congress Cataloging-in-Publication Data**
Mardell, Ben.
    From basketball to the Beatles : in search of compelling early
childhood curriculum / Ben Mardell : foreword by Eleanor Duckworth.
        p.   cm.
    Includes bibliographical references.
    ISBN 0-325-00194-4
    1. Early childhood education—United States—Curricula.
    2. Education, Preschool—United States—Curricula.   I. Title.
LB1139.4.M27   1999
372.19—dc21                                    99-26649
                                                  CIP

Editor: Lois Bridges
Production: Vicki Kasabian
Cover drawing: Mariah Thornton
Cover design: Jenny Jensen Greenleaf
Manufacturing: Louise Richardson

Printed in the United States of America on acid-free paper
03   02   01   00   99     MV     1   2   3   4   5

*In memory of Ricanne Hadrian*
*(1960 – 1996)*

# Contents

# Foreword

**ELEANOR DUCKWORTH**
School of Education, Harvard University

B en Mardell, a fine day-care teacher and the author of this intriguing book, writes of engaging his three- and four-year-old students in "formal study"—a thought that, initially, took me by surprise. I have always taken the work of day-care teachers seriously; but I had not, until reading this book, thought of it as entailing formal study.

And then, as a science educator, I was perplexed to see that, nonetheless, in and out of the "formal study" wove an astonishing degree of fantasy. When Mardell engages his students in a study of astronomy, the classroom loft becomes an observatory; children look through pretend telescopes and discover new planets. And when the children turn their attention to a study of real squirrels, a puppet baby squirrel appears in the classroom, so, as Mardell explains, "we can take care of it."

My mind went back to the beginnings of my work in science education. Together with Mike Savage I visited the first-grade science classroom of Kaki Aldrich. I remember that Mike and I left that visit rather daunted. With six-year-olds, it seemed, anything goes. No evidence seemed to rule out any generalization. How could one develop systematic understanding? (I had not until then quite fathomed the implications of the Inhelder and Piaget accounts that small children are perfectly happy to have a different explanation for every event: this floats because it is small; this floats because it is made of plastic; this floats because it is heavy and strong enough to hold itself up—and so on, with no need at all for a unifying principle.) I witnessed one grand truth about teaching science to that age when Aldrich took a group to the Boston Children's Museum. They were seated around her on the floor talking about something when she suddenly drew in her breath, asked them in a hushed voice to be VERY quiet, and drew their attention to—a fly, a housefly, walking on the floor. If they were VERY still, she whispered, it wouldn't fly away, and they could watch it. They were, and it didn't, and they did—with awe. That was a superb lesson for a budding science teacher.

This book, about three- and four-year-olds, has lessons for me of a different sort. It is the interplay of fantasy and reality that captivates me this time.

ix

Mardell knows a lot about the subjects in which he engages the children. One of the challenges my graduate students always face is: other than simply telling your students everything you know, what else do you, as a teacher, do with your knowledge? Ben Mardell cannot avoid that challenge: there is clearly no point in his telling these children everything he knows. Instead, he draws on what he knows to find ways of engaging them in paying attention to and thinking about these subjects.

And this book has helped me see that here is where the fantasy comes into play. Fantasy is the way to engage three- and four-year-olds in "formal study" of the real world and how it works. To initiate the study of South Africa, Mardell read the children a letter, supposedly sent to them by a young character in a book they were familiar with, inviting them to come on a safari to see wild animals. "The preschoolers packed their suitcases, and after a twelve-hour flight were met at the Cape Town airport. The preschoolers and their host then boarded a Land Rover and headed off on safari to Auginbies Falls National Park . . . " Their engagement was developed in the block area, in a nearby outdoor green space, in dramatic play, in a zoological museum, through more story books and letters. They became children of South Africa, wild animals, drummers, dancers, beadworkers, and, eventually, Nelson Mandela. Mardell had noticed that "while they absorb the respect that adults give to him, no one ever wants to be Dr. King in dramatic play. No preschooler wants to be killed at the end of the story. On the other hand, everyone wanted to be Nelson Mandela." And this because of the way Mardell was able to appeal to their intense feelings about fairness.

Mardell's South Africa curriculum investigates and examines Mandela's life and work. And then, the children's understanding of South Africa and Mandela comes back to play a role in their own classroom interactions. "The preschoolers had a new hero, a hero whose standards for justice and equality," Mardell writes, "provided them a moral compass in their own search for fairness." This is another truth that becomes clear in this book. Curriculum that works for three- and four-year-olds stays with them, in and out of their school year, and I am sure, beyond. This is because, as Mardell makes clear, making curriculum "work" for preschoolers demands that it involve their hearts and souls, their passions and fantasies. There is no other way.

Also evident are the ways in which Mardell fully embraces subject matters. Fantasy is central, but he doesn't allow it to run away with the study. The children were used to playing at being squirrels. This time, "along with imagining they were squirrels, I wanted the children to imagine (and become) people who studied squirrels."

He involves stories, art, and song, both as means of engagement, and as varied mediums for expressing what the children are learning and feeling.

He also must attend to needs of specific children whose feelings about the world and the people in it do not leave them free to bring themselves wholeheartedly to their work.

And with all his mastery of this most complex of professions—teaching children—Mardell is open about the ways in which he is still learning. So the book does not leave us awestruck by the brilliance of a single teacher. It draws us in, to see how important this work is, what it can look like when it is done well, and to think that we have understood something about young children so that we, too, might engage their hearts and souls, their passions and fantasies.

# Acknowledgments

This book is the fruit of several years' work as the afternoon preschool teacher at the Oxford Street Day Care Cooperative. I want to thank the staff at Oxford Street—Tavia Mead, Paul Ketterer, Alemishet Kidane, Vasantha Sooriar, Janet Crowley, Agnes Lugira, Aren Stone, Maggie Ashton, Kim Roux, and Cathy Craddock—for making the center a wonderful place to teach. In particular I want to thank Cathy Craddock, my co-teacher, for helping make coming to work each day a pleasure. I also want to acknowledge several very talented student teachers, Jackie Rosenbloom, Deborah Freeman, Sarah Marcus, Jenn Carlson, Kevin Clark, Jenny Stock, Darlene Campbell-Powell, and Chantal Lesdesma, for bringing fresh perspectives and analysis into my classroom.

Many of the ideas presented here were first discussed in my writing group. The insights, support, and friendship offered by Anne Kornblatt, the group's other member, helped make this book a reality.

As this volume took shape, the input of several friends and colleagues was invaluable. My thanks to my sisters, Ruth and Dina Mardell, and to Jackie Rosenbloom, Rebecca Keebler, Bobbi Rosenquest, Marc Kenen, Sandra Wilde, Patrick Shannon, and Cynthia Tyson for reading drafts of the essays which follow. In this vein, the supportive comments of my editor, Lois Bridges, helped improve the quality of this work in many ways.

Finally, I want to thank my wife, Liz Merrill. For the past dozen years Liz's patient counsel on the dilemmas of teaching has been my reality check. Her encouragement, support, and critical readings of innumerable drafts were invaluable to this project. Most important, she made coming home each evening even more fun than being at work.

# "All You Need Is Love": An Introduction

The year is 1967. President Johnson sends another 100,000 American troops to Vietnam. College campuses in the United States and Western Europe are rocked by violent protests. War erupts in the Middle East. And the Beatles, in the first-ever global television broadcast, sing their new tune, "All You Need Is Love." In this premiere, the Four Lads from Liverpool send their audience of 400,000,000 a very timely message.

The year is 1999. Educational conferences are filled with sessions describing how to scaffold young children's cognitive development. Bookstores feature titles proclaiming, "What Your Preschooler Needs to Know." Policy makers focus on young children's possession of specific skills as indicators of their readiness to learn. And I, after much thought, title the introduction to my book on early child curriculum, "All You Need Is Love." Given the current climate in educational discourse, mine is also a timely message.

I begin these chapters on early childhood curriculum by highlighting love because the term is seldom mentioned in serious discussions of early childhood education. When love is referred to at all, it is with regard to the fact that we are a caring profession. Love's role in teaching and learning is ignored. Indeed, when educators divide up the world, love and curriculum are placed into separate domains: love in the emotional realm, and curriculum in the cognitive sphere. Yet this separation denies an essential truth: for curriculum to be truly successful a good measure of love must be present.

What's love got to do with it? In a real sense, everything. When I bring my loves—my interests and passions—into the classroom I am able to convey a genuine enthusiasm for the topic at hand. This enthusiasm is the elixir that turns ordinary activities into compelling curriculum. If I hit upon an area that the children love—or come to love—we become bound together by our common interest. The classroom becomes a place where study and discovery are celebrated. And in the end it is this love of learning in general and passion for specific content areas that we are trying to nourish in our charges. Love and wonder are the seeds of knowledge that will help children blossom into lifelong learners.

The role love plays is most apparent during those times when curriculum units are going well. These times are marked by a shared excitement about learning that permeates the classroom. Such an atmosphere filled my classroom during our study of the Beatles. I love the Beatles' music, and on noticing that several children were interested in the band, I introduced a unit on the Fab Four. The results were electrifying as Beatlemania struck the classroom. Playing "The Beatles" became the class' favorite activity as children walked around belting out Beatles' tunes and vied for the roles of John, Paul, George, and Ringo. We excitedly discussed important moments in the band's history as well as the instrumentation on favorite songs. I was thrilled by the children's complete devotion to a unit of study. It became abundantly clear to me that in the search for compelling early childhood curriculum, "all you need is love."

This book is written for those who love helping young children learn. I hope the essays that follow will both entertain and edify the reader. First, the chapters describe specific curriculum, group-time activities, art projects, and field trips undertaken to help children explore various topics of study. Topics range from squirrels to storytelling, astronomy to South Africa, and basketball to the Beatles. The curriculum has been field-tested in my work with three groups of preschoolers at the Oxford Street Day Care Cooperative in Cambridge, Massachusetts.

Second, embedded in the essays are some guiding principles on curriculum development and implementation that I have evolved over the past fifteen years of teaching young children, including

- using stories to bring topics of study to life;
- tapping children's fantasy and play to further inquiry;
- observing children in order to understand their interests and guide their activities;
- teaching skills as a natural part of study;
- inculcating a culture of study to build a community of learners;
- extending the learning environment beyond the classroom; and
- understanding teaching as a dynamic process involving experimentation, reflection, and continual revision.

Of course, the importance of love in curriculum is the thread that runs throughout the book.

The book begins with a chapter about a curriculum unit undertaken early in the year. "Begin by Studying What's Around: Squirrels" details an investigation of the rodent family *Sciuridae* and shows how the investigation helped my students get started studying. With Chapter 2, "Reaching for the Stars: Astronomy," I skip ahead to January. The temporal gap is not coincidental, as most compelling curriculum does not occur until several months into the year, after the children have grown accustomed to undertaking explorations. Chapter 3, "Hoop Dreams: Basketball," focuses on another winter unit—two seasons of studying my favorite sport. The essay highlights the role of fantasy and play in children's investigations of the world.

During the year it is not only curriculum that occupies our time. "The Case of Miss D.: Emotions" is the story of how my co-teacher Cathy and I struggled to help a little girl better function in the classroom so that she could participate in the curriculum. Of course, for all students, cognitive development is not the sole focus. Chapter 5, "In Search of Fairness: South Africa," takes up the issue of moral education. Chapter 6, "And We Told Wonderful Stories Also: Storytelling," describes the important role of storytelling in my literacy program and in early childhood classrooms. The final chapter describes a unit that took place at the end of the year. "Sgt. Pepper and Beyond: The Beatles, the Talking Heads, and the Preschool Band" discusses how I, a nonmusician, explored music with my students.

As an Ivy League graduate with a Ph.D., I sometimes have a difficult time explaining to family, friends, and acquaintances why I continue to be a day care teacher. In their less sympathetic moments, they are still waiting for me to get "a real job." Even the supervisor of a student teacher, a former teacher herself, once quipped, "You're certainly overqualified for this job." The short explanation about my chosen profession is that I love my work, but I sense a more extensive explanation would be helpful. This book is my more extensive explanation. I hope the challenge, excitement, and joy of teaching is apparent in these chapters. I hope the book conveys to readers why teaching continues to fascinate me after a decade and a half on the job. And I hope to convince readers of the timeliness and necessity of including love in a serious discussion of early childhood education.

# 1

## *Begin by Studying What's Around: Squirrels*

### The Dead Squirrel: Part 1

Never in my wildest imagination did I consider that my preschool class' study of squirrels would lead me to the Mammalian Department at Harvard University's Museum of Comparative Zoology. But there I stood, among cabinets containing mouse skeletons, elephant skulls, chipmunk skins, and polar bear pelts, discussing with Judy Chupasko the possibility of her visiting my classroom to skin and stuff our dead squirrel.

My encounter with the dead squirrel started in complete innocence three days into my class' study of squirrels. As I was walking my son Sam to kindergarten, we came upon a deceased squirrel lying by the side of the road. A cursory examination revealed that the carcass was well preserved. Though I wasn't exactly sure what to do with it and despite some squeamishness about picking it up, I sensed the cadaver had potential as a teaching tool, so I scooped it into a shopping bag and, on my return home, popped it into the freezer.

At this point in the story, most people exclaim, "Oh gross!" That's what my sister Dina said when I told her what I had in the shopping bag. That's what my co-teacher Cathy said when I informed her of my find. That and more is what my wife Liz said when I warned her to be careful when she opened the freezer.

Undeterred, even buoyed, by these comments (I hadn't grossed out my sister in years), I contacted the pest control department of a local university to make sure there were no communicable diseases harbored by dead squirrels. Dr. Gary Alpert returned my call the next day. "It's good you phoned," he began, "because there are animals whose carcasses transmit disease. Fortunately, the gray squirrel of Eastern Massachusetts is not among these at present." I proceeded to learn from Dr. Alpert that in freezing the animal I had killed any fleas or parasites that might have made this particular squirrel their host. Then he took the conversation in an unexpected direction. Unfazed by my collection of the squirrel, he was quite enthusiastic. "This is a great potential learning tool. It's so hard for children to get up close to wild animals. Your squirrel could provide a unique opportunity for careful observation and study. Would you," he asked, "be interested in having the squirrel prepared for scientific study?" Gary explained this meant its fur would be preserved and its bones removed for examination. He had a friend at the Museum of Comparative Zoology who might be willing to undertake the project.

Which brought me to the Mammalian Department and my meeting with Judy Chupasko. Judy's work involves the preparation of animals used in scientific study. "You know," she confided, "when I tell people what I do for my job they usually respond, "Oh, gross." I inadvertently smiled as she continued:

> It's a sign of how out of touch we are with the natural world. Even a few generations ago most people would have had experience either killing animals or preparing dead animals for food. Today, just the sight of a dead animal is considered repellent.

I nodded in agreement, not disclosing the fact that I'm a vegetarian. She proceeded:

> But kids haven't been socialized yet into being grossed out by this stuff. They are really fascinated by dead animals. They want to know what's inside, where the bones are, what the muscles look like, and so on. And the fact that the animal is dead, well, that's just part of nature.

I agreed, and we set a date for Judy to visit. A few weeks later she was in my classroom with a scalpel, scissors, needle and thread, cotton batting, and a box of corn meal. Around her sat a dozen attentive children. In front of them was the now defrosted dead squirrel.

## Welcome to the Preschool Room

Welcome to the sometimes wild, occasionally wacky, and often wonderful world of preschool. While not every unit of study in my room leads to such unexpected adventures, when my class and I delve into a topic the results are unpredictable and frequently exciting.

While I would humbly describe the goings-on inside my preschool room as compelling curriculum, the physical space where these adventures occur is rather pedestrian. Exposed pipes hang from the ceiling. The walls are in need of repainting. The furniture is a mismatched collection of used and home-made shelving, tables, and chairs. Like many day cares in the United States, my center is strapped for cash and housed in a structure not intended for young children. The building's first occupant, the Army ROTC, was forced to leave by a social ferment that led the center's landlord, a prominent university, to make space available for child care. Ironically, these days boxes of toys occupy shelves originally intended for rifles.

Despite the center's physical limitations, Cathy and I have worked hard to create a comfortable, stimulating environment for children. Typical of many early childhood settings, our preschool room is organized into play areas or learning centers. Entering the L-shaped classroom one immediately encounters a dramatic play area, which is often stocked with dress-up clothes and kitchen equipment. Above the dramatic play area is the loft, a secluded seven-foot-by-seven-foot multipurpose space that can be reached only by climbing a ladder. Adjoining dramatic play is a carpeted block area, used for Legos, Lincoln Logs, and a large collection of wooden unit blocks. Adjacent to the block area are the sand and water tables. Continuing through the room there is a round table used for used puzzles and small manipulative toys, lunch, and snacks. At the corner of the ell is the book area, home to group meetings and quiet reading. Turning the corner there is a long table, around which a dozen children can squeeze. To facilitate art projects, child-accessible shelves neighboring the table hold an assortment of paper, markers, pencils, crayons, scissors, glue, tape dispensers, and staplers. Two easels on the wall bordering the long table complete the room (see Figure 1–1).

In contrast to the physical environment, the center's organizational structure is anything but typical. A product of the social idealism of the 1960s, the center is a parent-staff cooperative. Policies, including tuition and salaries, are made by consensus (a process where everyone must accept a decision for it to be passed) at meetings open to all parents and teachers. There is an administrator, not a director, with the nine staff members participating in peer supervision. The curriculum described in this book was conceived within this egalitarian culture. While not directly linked to the center's organizational structure, my creativity has flourished in this work environment.

As part of their cooperative responsibilities, parents take turns as the "parent helper," serving as the class' assistant teacher. A second adult is always in the classroom to help Cathy in the morning and me, in the afternoon, care for our twelve charges. By the time they reach the Preschool Room, some have done their parent help once a week for three years. They have seen their children grow up together and have experienced the joys and hardships of

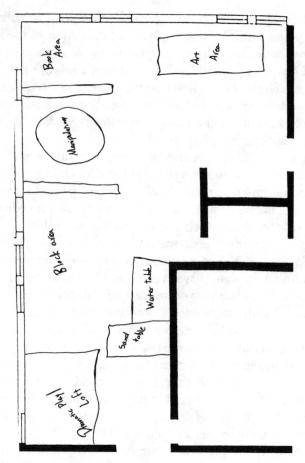

Figure 1–1. *Floor plan*

parenting with the other adults in the group. The children also experience this sense of group. Having been together from babyhood, they come to feel they are part of an extended family. This sense of community is a defining characteristic of the center. It is a feeling that Cathy and I try to nurture each year as children from the Stomper Room (three-year-olds) come together with repeat preschoolers and new admissions to form our preschooler group.

A challenge in community building is the diversity of our groups. Because of the center's urban location and proximity to several universities, the students of the Preschool Room come from the four corners of the globe. Approximately one-third of the children in the room in a given year speak a language other than English at home. During the past three years, our population has included Haitian, Columbian, Italian, English, French, Swiss,

Spanish, Israeli, Chinese, Japanese, Korean, and Nigerian families. While the majority of these children come from well-educated backgrounds, several state-subsidized slots add socioeconomic diversity to the mix.

Cathy opens our mini–United Nations at 8:15 A.M. I arrive for my shift at 12:30 P.M. During the next five hours I will tell a story (12:45–1:00), help children rest during a state-mandated nap time (1:00–1:45), supervise outdoor free play and quiet indoor projects (1:45–3:00), lead a group meeting (3:00–3:20), serve snack (3:20–3:30), take the children on a walk (3:30–4:15), facilitate an exploration time (4:15–5:15), and run a final story time to end the day (5:15–5:30). My day will also include tying many pairs of shoes, settling disputes, comforting children missing their parents, along with helping them learn about the world.

## Why Squirrels?

"Now what?" That was the question Cathy and I were mulling over during our weekly team meeting. The "what" in our question referred to the curriculum.

It was the first week of October, and we were pleased to have survived September. For preschool teachers, September is a grueling month. Orienting a gaggle of confused three- and four-year-olds to a new classroom, new classmates, and new routines is a Herculean task. For a month straight we define terms ("The Preschool Room ends here at the doorway"), set expectations ("No, you can't stand on the table"), and provide patient explanations to worried children ("Your mother will pick you up at the end of the day"). The job is made more difficult by the fact that the children acutely miss their parents and pine for their former teachers and, as a result, often act oppositionally to suggestions made by the new and unfamiliar adults in their lives (in this case Cathy and me). But we had done it—oriented our new group. Each of our new students now knew where their cubbies were, what their classmates' and teachers' names were, and what to do with their cup after snack. With the basics of the classroom mastered, we were ready for something more. We were ready for curriculum, for our first unit of study.

Cathy and I organize our curriculum into units of study. During these one- to four-week time periods many of the classroom activities revolve around a common theme. For example, when we study birds many of our songs, art projects, and stories connect to the avian world. Organizing curriculum in this manner provides coherence to activities and helps children develop their identity as learners. The children incorporate the idea of studying a particular topic into their self-concept of "preschoolerhood." Quite frequently, the first question a child asks upon returning from a vacation is

"What are we studying?" This identity as a learner/studier has tremendous implications for the curriculum.

By October I am more than ready to begin units of study. I find that I don't really get to know, or fully appreciate, a new group until we study together. Preceding units of study, I experience new children as usurpers who have displaced my beloved former students. Once study begins, however, we become partners involved in an exciting endeavor. We get to know each other. We begin to appreciate each other. We become attached. Philosopher David Hawkins (1974) explains this phenomenon well, describing content as an essential ingredient in the teacher-student relationship. Only by pursing common interests, by building what Hawkins calls "a community of subject matter and engagement," do child-teacher bonds form. Through units of study I learn essential information about my new students: what kind of investigators, artists, players, and storytellers they are. I suspect something complementary occurs for my students. By helping them learn new competencies, guiding them to places they hadn't been before, and captivating them with activities and subject matter, the children get to know and value me. The curriculum becomes the basis upon which we build our communication. This communication takes place on a new and exciting plane for preschoolers, a plane imbued with importance and dignity.

Which brings me back to Cathy's and my question, "Now what?" Our search for curriculum units often begins by trying to identify the children's interests. Because three- and four-year-olds are hard put to articulate their interests, especially at the beginning of the year when the concept of studying is just emerging, this process involves some detective work. Most of our clues come from the children's play, which serves as an excellent indicator of their interests. Comparing notes, Cathy and I had both observed a great deal of animal play, much of it loosely based on the then-popular Disney film *The Lion King*. We had witnessed playground battles between lions and hyenas, chimpanzees swinging on the climbing structure, and an occasional cheetah darting across the play yard, and had considered units on lions or on African animals in general as possibilities.

But these options weren't quite right. We were in Massachusetts, and it wasn't often that one encountered a lion or hyena. For our initial unit I wanted a more immediate topic, something the children could observe and interact with. I wanted to study something that was around us. Gazing out the window at a gray squirrel scurrying up a tree, I blurted, "How about squirrels?" Though I made the comment in jest, Cathy thought it was a good idea. Further consideration convinced us that I had inadvertently hit upon something with great potential.

The resulting unit was a resounding success. Cathy and I learned that squirrels have lots of what David Hawkins refers to as "surface area"—many ways for children to engage in the topic. Two years later we repeated the study of squirrels with another group of children who also displayed a strong interest in animals. What follows is a description of that study year. Embedded in the description are thoughts about:

- how stories can help bring a topic of study to life;
- how play can be utilized in the service of study; and
- how skills can be taught as a natural part of investigation.

The chapter also demonstrates how studying something around us prepared us to study objects that are light years away.

## The Baby Squirrel

It is the inaugural day of the squirrel unit, the first time this group of children and I will be studying a topic together and, for some of the children, the first time they will be involved in any formal study.

I am anxious. How will the children respond to squirrels? Does this group have the inclination and capacity, the attention span and intellectual curiosity, to become deeply involved in units of study? The fate of our year revolves around these questions.

Since beginnings set the tone for what comes next, I want to capture the children's attention immediately, welcoming them into the world of study. My plan is to begin where the children's hearts are by linking squirrels to a central issue in their lives: separation from their parents. To do so I have a story involving children and their parents, separation, danger, and ultimately, deliverance.

Several years ago I witnessed a riveting scene involving some gray squirrels. I based my story on this scene, making it contemporary, and embellishing the ending in order to involve the children. I told my audience at our prenap meeting:

> This morning I saw something truly amazing. I was standing on my porch when I noticed that almost all the cats in the neighborhood had gathered around the blue spruce tree in my yard. They were meowing very loudly and looking up at the top of the tree. I went over to the spruce to take a closer look. From up in the tree I heard squeaking and chattering. Then a mother squirrel appeared. She was holding a baby in her mouth the way cats do, by the scruff of its neck. Like a bolt of lightening, the mom raced down

the tree, past the cats, across the yard, and up a maple tree. Then she disappeared into a hole. It all happened so quickly the cats didn't know what hit them. And then it happened again! This time the father squirrel raced down the spruce carrying a baby, and brought it over to the hole in the maple tree.

I went on to describe how the squirrel parents made several more trips from the spruce to the maple, spiriting out six more babies to their new nest. But then, with one baby remaining in the old nest:

> The parents didn't come back, and from the top of the tree I could hear the sad cries of the one last baby. It was all alone. It sounded very scared. The baby was waiting for its parents, but they never returned.

As I told about the abandoned baby there were looks of great concern on the children's faces. Jessie, whose father was overseas for several months on business, seemed particularly upset and looked like she was going to cry. Tears were spared when I gave the story a Hollywoodesque ending, explaining how I had climbed the spruce, rescued the baby, and brought it into my house. A giant smile emerged on Jessie's face when I reached into my backpack and pulled out the baby squirrel. While the "baby" I held up was actually a puppet, the children took this leap from the real to the imaginary in stride. They clamored for a turn to hold the adorable creature, and were delighted when I informed them that "as part of our studying squirrels, the baby will live in our class so we can take care of it."

The children's first opportunity to care for our newly adopted squirrel came later that afternoon. One of the exploration choices was feeding and caring for the baby. Jessie, Sean, and Shoshana went up to the loft, where there was a baby bottle, blankets, and pillows. They conscientiously fed and swaddled the puppet while Jason, Aviva, and Eduardo clamored for a turn to provide assistance. The next day at meeting we brainstormed names for the baby. Caretaking was again a popular exploration time activity. The baby squirrel had won the children's hearts.

Even more significant to my efforts to inculcate a culture of study among the new preschoolers, squirrels in general began to win the children's minds. Squirrels replaced hyenas and bats as the roles children took in their outdoor play. The change emerged on the second day of the squirrel unit. As Scott was getting his coat on to go outside, he turned to his usual playmates, Pierce, Jerry, and Eduardo, and suggested, "Let's play squirrels!" Once outside not only Scott and his mates, but the entire group became involved in squirrel play. They gathered food, hid from imaginary predators, cared for their young, and carried leaves up into the climbing structure to make nests. Needless to say, I was very pleased about this sign that the curriculum was engaging the children.

The squirrel unit was just a few days old, but already I had learned a great deal about this group of children. Like most groups of preschoolers I've encountered, they were players, effortlessly and enthusiastically embracing stories and drama. More unusual, but very encouraging, was that they were very open to adult initiative in their play. I had offered the theme of squirrels, and they were off and running.

Once we discovered the group's openness to incorporating adult initiatives into their fantasies, the question became where, if anywhere, to steer the children's play. One possibility was to embellish the squirrel play by providing bushy tails, suggesting more extensive squirrel habitats, and telling additional baby squirrel stories. I decided against this. The squirrel play occurring resembled the previous hyena play in many ways. Just as they had as hyenas, as squirrels the children took care of babies, gathered food, and were chased by predators. While involving squirrels on a superficial level, the focus of the play lay in the larger issues of caretaking and survival. Moreover, the children were content with their squirrel play, and did not need adult input to sustain it.

I decided to capitalize on the children's openness to suggestion in their play by expanding the play roles the children were taking. Along with imagining they were squirrels, I wanted the children to imagine (and become) people who *studied* squirrels. I wanted them to become squirrel scientists.

## Squirrel Scientists

Featuring tree-lined residential streets, the neighborhood around the day care center is home to a robust squirrel population. Before we began our unit, the occasional squirrel that wandered across the play yard would raise mild interest. With our study of squirrels begun, squirrel sightings created great excitement.

To take advantage of this local resource and meld the children's proclivity to play with my desire to have them learn, I ordained the preschoolers "Squirrel Scientists." The children received the news as they were seated in the play yard in preparation for our daily walk. As squirrel scientists, I explained in a serious tone, "One of your jobs is to find out how many squirrels live around the day care center. The way to do this is to take a census." I held up a two-by-three-foot sheet of oak tag, and continued:

> We'll use this piece of paper to take our census, marking down all the squirrels we notice. All the squirrels we see in the yard, or out the window, or on our walks we'll mark down. When we're finished we'll know how many squirrels live in the day care neighborhood.

After a brief safety message about interacting with squirrels, the squirrel scientists were off to "the woods," a half-acre oasis of grass and trees in the midst of the city. On the way to the woods, Pierce spied a squirrel. I offered enthusiastic congratulations, and dramatically marked the sighting on my clipboard. Jerry then called out that he too had seen a squirrel. I congratulated him as well, and marked down the sighting. In all, the children noticed five squirrels on the way to the woods. The woods themselves, however, were devoid of squirrels. Without anything to observe, the squirrel scientists soon took on other roles, becoming pirates and bridesmaids. On our return to the day care center I gathered the children together. Solemnly marking off the five sightings on the base-ten grid outlined on the census paper, I commended the scientists for a productive first day of counting.

For the next few days I began each walk by reviewing the census. I hoped the importance with which I regarded the activity would spread. It did. By the third day of census taking Pierce was encouraging his friends to "keep our eyes out for squirrels." They did. Arriving at day care on the next day, Jason reported how he had seen two squirrels that morning. That afternoon Scott came in from the play yard to report a squirrel sighting. Over the next few days I heard from Jerry and Sean about squirrels seen near home, and from Aviva about an albino squirrel she had seen during a trip to New York City. Squirrels, it seemed, were all around. After the first week we had counted, and no doubt double- and triple-counted, forty-five squirrels.

In theory, the census could have been undertaken by preschoolers instead of squirrel scientists. In practice, the importance of the fantasy overlay should not be underestimated. Even for young children, who have little understanding of what a scientist is, the word conjures up something powerful, even magical. Framing the census as a scientific undertaking imbued it with a sense of gravity and worth. It also provided a reference point for other activities. When I asked the children to become squirrel scientists, they knew something of importance was about to occur.

I made use of this reference point during the second week of the unit when I asked the squirrel scientists to estimate a final census total. Prepared for a wide variety of answers, I was still surprised by the children's responses. Pierce answered first. "Four," he told me with great seriousness. Because Pierce was rightly perceived as an expert with numbers, Scott and Eduardo, who answered next, predicted four as well. Aviva then weighed in. Proving to be an independent thinker, she estimated seven. In all, guesses ranged from a high of seven to a low of two. The conversation sent the parent helper into a state of near hysterics at the contradiction between the already sighted forty-five squirrels and the children's predictions. Despite the humor of the situation, I kept a straight face, acknowledging and validating, but not evaluating, each answer.

My rationale for not correcting the children's wrong answers is straightforward. I was asking the children to take a significant risk by voicing an opinion about an issue of some complexity. For many in the class, voicing such opinions was new. Some might not even have known they had an opinion. We were at a fledgling stage of children sharing their ideas and thoughts with the group. It was critical that I take each child's answer seriously without passing judgment. If this conversation had occurred later in the year, when children were more secure in venturing opinions, I might have pointed out that we had passed the number four in the census. For now, I was pleased the children were willing to hazard any answer. Four was as good a response as one hundred and four.

The census taking continued over the next ten days, now almost completely sustained by the children's initiative. Perhaps the most interesting sightings occurred at the squirrel feeder, a wooden platform I placed outside the meeting area window. Loaded with birdseed, the feeder attracted several gray squirrels each day. Protected by the window screen, the squirrels were unfazed by our proximity (only a few feet away), and the children had a wonderful opportunity to watch them eat, climb, and eventually gnaw apart the plastic bowl where their food was kept. The children insisted that we mark the feeder's visitors on the census chart.

Of course, squirrel scientists do more than take censuses. They also know a lot about squirrels. To help get the children up to speed on the canon of squirrel knowledge, I sprinkled my conversations with squirrel facts, including:

- The gray squirrel's primary food is acorns, while red squirrels subsist on conifer seeds;
- Gray and red squirrels are excellent swimmers. Their cousins, the flying squirrels, face certain death if they accidently land in the water;
- Flying squirrels are nocturnal. By contrast, gray squirrels are diurnal, and are most active in the morning and in the late afternoon.

And my favorite squirrel fact:

- Squirrel species are distributed worldwide, though there are no squirrels in Australia or Madagascar.

In their identity as squirrel scientists, the children eagerly gobbled up this trivia. Pierce, Scott, and Jerry, particularly, enjoyed sharing these facts with adults, relishing their possession of the treasured commodity of information. Just saying these new words, *nocturnal, diurnal,* and *Madagascar,* gave the children great pleasure. It was the enjoyment of knowing and sharing knowledge, not the memorization of specific facts, that was of value here.

Being a scientist involves much more than knowing information. Scientists also discuss ideas and debate theories. Participating in such scientific discourse is a challenging task, requiring practice. Wanting to learn what the children were capable of and give them some practice in such discussions, I posed the question, Do squirrels eat snakes? This question originated in a conversation that occurred on the very first day of our studying squirrels. I asked the children what they wanted to know about squirrels. Shoshana wondered, "What do squirrels eat?" Aviva, who was gazing at a photograph of a squirrel confronting a snake by its burrow, responded, "They eat snakes." There were some murmurs of disagreement, but no time to pursue the issue. We returned to the question at a meeting two weeks later when I asked:

*Ben:* So, squirrel scientists, we've been learning about what squirrels eat by watching what they take from the feeder. We've found out they eat nuts, pumpkin meat, and muffins. One question we haven't answered yet that some children raised a few weeks ago is: Do squirrels eat snakes?

*Shoshana:* No.

*Ben:* Why do you say that?

*Shoshana:* Because they eat chestnuts.

*Ben:* Ah, so they don't eat meat. Jessie, what do you think?

*Jessie:* No.

*Ben:* Why not?

*Jessie:* Because they eat acorns.

These were very reasonable responses, though I worried the conversation might end here. To provoke some debate, I asked:

*Ben:* OK, so some of you scientists think squirrels *don't* eat snakes. Does anyone *disagree* with this? Does anyone think that squirrels *do* eat snakes?

*Jerry:* I think they eat snakes.

*Ben:* Why?

*Jerry:* Because [a] gray [squirrel] has sharp teeth.

*Ben:* So that means it might be a meat eater. Pierce, do you agree with Jerry?

*Pierce:* Yes, because flying squirrels are up at night.

*Ben:* So . . . ?

*Pierce:* Like owls.

*Ben:* Oh, so they eat snakes like owls do?

*Pierce:* Yeah.

*Ben:* Aviva, do you think squirrels eat snakes or not?

*Aviva:* They do.

*Ben:* Why do you say that?

*Aviva:* Because I've seen the picture.

The pro-snake-eating position presented, I encouraged the anti-snake-eating side to respond. Shoshana and Jessie restated their ideas, though they did not address Jerry, Pierce, or Aviva's arguments. I was impressed that the children could articulate a rationale to support their opinions, but curious that they had little inclination to argue. Unlike other groups I've worked with, who became passionate in such discussions, these children were content to state their opinions and move on.

Near the end of our squirrel unit Max, a preschool alum, paid a visit to the class. During the review of the census, which was at seventy-three squirrels, Max raised his hand and proudly announced, "When we studied squirrels we counted eighty-eight." Checking my records that evening I found that Max's recollection of two years before was accurate. Census taking had certainly made an impression on him, and now the new group of preschoolers/squirrel scientists had a record to beat.

The record, however, was not on the group's mind when we returned to the woods on the last day of studying squirrels. The children immediately became involved in a variety of play: weddings, Winnie-the-Pooh, and the Titanic. But unlike our first visit, on this day the neighborhood squirrels also converged on the woods en masse. It was as if they knew this was their last chance and decided to put on a show. It began with chattering up at the tops of the trees, then the squirrels scurried down and jumped across the children's paths. Acrobatic leaps from tree to tree followed. The display pulled the children out of their wedding and boat fantasies, and with a gentle cue from me ("Squirrel scientists, what do you think about this!!?"), they assumed their scientific roles, observed the squirrels' behavior, chased them through the woods, and of course, counted. When Pierce, Scott, and Jerry remembered that they were nearing the previous census record, the counting took on some urgency. In total, the children recorded thirty squirrels. We returned to the day care center for the final census tally. There was undivided attention as I marked off the day's find. A cheer went up as the count hit eighty-nine. As it passed one hundred Sean gasped. The final count was one hundred and eleven. I suspected that some of the squirrel scientists would remember this number for a long time.

## Fun with Squirrels

Taking on the identity of squirrel scientists was a heady experience for the children. They were particularly proud of their census work. And work it was. Taking the census, observing their activities, and studying and discussing their eating habits were clearly framed as serious endeavors. But just as I wanted the children to experience the seriousness of study, I wanted them to have fun, too. I wanted them to sense the playful side of study, where connections between ideas and lighthearted activities are made. Throughout our three-week investigation we had fun with squirrels.

Fun for preschoolers often involves food; the shortest way to young children's hearts is through their stomach. During our study of squirrels' eating habits, we learned that the acorn forms the staple of the gray squirrel's diet, so I raised the idea of baking acorn muffins. I had heard about acorn muffins from my Cousin Seth, who is a wonderful source of interesting and unusual information. A few years ago he stopped by my house with some acorn muffins, which, as you might expect, had a delightfully nutty flavor. When I told the children about the muffins and Seth's recipe, they wanted to make some themselves. The recipe called for fifty white oak acorns. After a fruitless search in the neighborhood for a white oak tree, I mistakenly settled for a red oak. The children enthusiastically gathered the acorns and we soon reached our quota.

I decided to use exploration time to allow the children to test the hardness of acorn shells and to extract the nut meat. With two-thirds of the group squeezed around a table, I handed an acorn to each child and asked them to remove the shell. After some squeezing and pounding, most expressed frustration. Pierce was the most enterprising—and squirrel-like. Escaping my attention, he quietly used his teeth to bore a small hole in the shell. The point of hardness made, and wanting to preserve Pierce's teeth, I passed out small hammers to aid with the task. What followed was the kind of activity preschoolers thrive on—one imbued with a sense of purpose where they physically alter the world. With some initial help the children were able to crack the acorns. Scott laughed with delight each time he freed the meat from the shell. Deborah looked as if she were doing brain surgery, so deep was her concentration. Then Shoshana discovered an acorn infested with a wasp larva. We discussed how both people and squirrels reject these rotten nuts. After thirty minutes of shelling, we boiled the meat to leach out the tannic acid.

I took the acorn meat home that evening, reboiling it several times for good measure. After drying it in a toaster oven, I sampled the fruit of our labor. My mouth contorted. It was like biting into a piece of horseradish, only much more bitter. In the hopes that my mouth was deceiving me, I took another taste. The results were the same. There was no denying it: the acorns were inedible.

The next day Scott and Pierce arrived at day care excitedly talking about baking acorn muffins. I knew I had to admit my mistake. I made my confession at meeting in the form of a story:

> The baby squirrel wanted to thank the preschoolers for taking such good care of him, so he decided to make them some acorn muffins. He gathered acorns, shelled them, ground them into flour, mixed in the other ingredients, and popped them in the oven to bake. When they were all done the squirrel proudly handed me one. They looked delicious. My mouth was watering as I got ready to take a bite.

I paused, dramatizing my anticipation as I brought an imaginary muffin to my mouth.

> But then: YUCK! The muffin tasted terrible. "What did you put in these things?" I yelled. After discussing the situation, the squirrel and I realized he had gotten the *wrong kind of acorns.* While squirrels love all kinds of acorns, people only like acorns from white oak trees. Acorns from red oak trees taste too bitter for people to eat.

I admitted that I too had gotten the wrong kind of acorns, and thus we couldn't go ahead with our plans to make acorn muffins. The children's disappointment was alleviated by the news that we could make walnut muffins instead.

From sustenance for the body, we proceeded to sustenance for the soul: music. Glancing through the newspaper the week before the squirrel unit began, I happened upon an article in the business section. Entitled "Striking a Chord: Hot Band of Today Takes Name of Candy Time Forgot," the article included a photo with the caption "hot selling band, the Squirrel Nut Zippers." *Squirrel* Nut Zippers! I read on. It seemed some musicians from North Carolina had named their group for a candy manufactured less than two miles from the day care center.

A coincidence like this could not be ignored. The Squirrel Nut Zippers had to be part of the squirrel unit. Through Kevin Clark, our student teacher, I obtained a Zipper CD. The music was toe-tapping good, something I thought the children would enjoy. Taking the liberty to interpret their music creatively, I introduced the Nut Zippers at a meeting time with a story:

> Last year, when you were in the Stomper Room, we had a problem with the trash cans outside. They were plastic, and a squirrel ate a hole right through

the top. After that, all the squirrels in the neighborhood were able to get into the trash can and eat the garbage. They would climb into the cans, looking for leftover snack. As they climbed out they'd make a huge mess. There would be garbage all over the parking lot. A band, the Squirrel Nut Zippers, knew something had to be done, so they wrote a song called "Put a Lid on It." And we did. Now there are metal tops on our garbage cans.

Snickering about a band called the Squirrel Nut Zippers and a song about garbage, we danced and played our harmonicas along with the Nut Zippers.

Our squirrel fun also included straight-out humor and spontaneous activities like "Silly Squirrels." As part of our information campaign, I had used a part of our meeting times to provide the children with data about different squirrel species. We discussed the common gray, red, and flying squirrels in depth, but I wanted to give a sense of the variety of squirrels. One day I mentioned eighteen other species (Abert, Chiriqui, Deppe's, Townstead, Southern Fox, Western Fox, Douglas Ground, Fischer Ground, Harris Ground, Richardson Ground, Golden Manteled Ground, Missouri Thirteen-Striped Ground, Golden Bellied, Colorado Rock, Lower Californian Antelope, Central American, European, and Japanese). Later, when I was about to revisit the gray squirrel, a crazy idea popped into my head. Spouting the nonsense preschoolers love, I said, "Now let's talk about the squirrel that has a long trunk and eats peanuts: the Elephant Squirrel." Hysterical laughter from the crowd. Inspired, I continued; "Now let's talk about the squirrel with sharp teeth that swims in the ocean: the Shark Squirrel." Hysterical laughter again. At this point, it was only fair to invite the children to have a turn. Pierce told of the Duck Squirrel that flaps its wings. Jerry introduced us to the Jim Squirrel that eats fish. Aviva mentioned the Cat Squirrel that lives in a shirt. Zealand concluded with the Pooky Squirrel that eats cookies.

It was a short step from our meeting-time hijinks to the *Silly Squirrel Book*. Inserted that day as an exploration time choice, I asked the children to draw a picture of their silly squirrel. After their pictures were completed, I asked each child a series of questions to elicit information normally found in animal guide books. Our *Silly Squirrel Book* read like a guide book. It was filled with species named after other animals and the children's mothers. Diets were diverse, ranging from other squirrels to airplane food. Habitats included the day care center and Africa. Most important, reading about these squirrels made the children hoot with laughter.

In having fun with squirrels I was learning what grabbed this group's attention. The children were seeing me try things out, make mistakes, and engage in flights of fancy. I was getting to know the children, and they were getting to know me. We were also learning a bit about squirrels.

# The Dead Squirrel: Part 2

Several years ago I found a dead sparrow on the play yard. When our intern Violet learned of the find she was horrified, insisting that the offending carcass be disposed of immediately. While I admired Violet's dedication to education, I found her to be overly protective of children, possessing a sanitized version of childhood. To expand her understanding of what children would find compelling, I placed the sparrow on the art table. Curriculumwise, this was a brilliant move. The bird drew the children like a magnet. We had wonderful conversations about bird anatomy and the role of death in nature, and the children produced spectacular observational drawings that day. So I knew, when I brought in the dead squirrel my son and I had found, that two reactions were likely: the children would be fascinated, and some adults would be appalled.

The children were fascinated. During the second week of the unit I brought the squirrel to a meeting time, placing it on display in the middle of our circle. After explaining how it was found, I invited the squirrel scientists to look closely at the specimen, asking them what they noticed. Their responses produced an inventory of body parts: claws, fur, a bushy tail, four legs, sharp teeth, and little ears.

At exploration time that afternoon eight children chose to draw the specimen. I began the activity by again asking the squirrel scientists what they noticed about the carcass. I then handed out paper. As they drew, the children chatted about the squirrel. Some of the conversations centered around the squirrel's death. Jessie wanted to know when and how it died. Jason, the youngest boy in the class, simply noted, "It's not moving." Sean solemnly told us, "It's not going to get alive again." No one expressed sadness about the squirrel's passing, or disgust about what they were drawing. These were scientists at work.

Their work varied between careful anatomical drawing to fairly random scribbling. Jessie and Jerry carefully drew a head, body, tail, and legs (see Figure 1–2). Zealand counted the legs and drew them, adding claws at the end of each. Aviva at first declared she was drawing a flying squirrel, ignoring the body in front of her. Eventually she looked at the specimen and, realizing she "forgot the whiskers," drew them in. Jason occasionally glanced at the squirrel as he drew seemingly random lines (see Figure 1–3).

I knew that the children's observational drawings would vary, just as the children's reactions to the project would differ. I knew my advanced drawers would closely observe the squirrel. I hoped they would use the specimen as a model from which to add greater detail to their work. I knew my less-skilled drawers wouldn't concern themselves with accuracy at all, and scribble away.

*Figure 1–2. Jerry's squirrel*

I hoped the squirrel would awaken them to the possibility of representational work. I knew my nondrawers, four boys who seemed allergic to pen-and-paper tasks, would stay away from the project. I hoped seeing their peers' excitement and my valuation might entice them to try drawing. Translating what they see onto a piece of paper is a challenging task, both conceptually and mechanically, for preschoolers. Part of my role as the teacher is to provide such challenges in supportive contexts. Like the predictions of the census' final tally, I regarded each picture positively.

The most exciting activity of our squirrel unit, the visit by Judy Chupasko, occurred a week after our formal study of squirrels concluded. I posted Judy's upcoming visit on the weekly calendar, explaining that "on Friday a grown-up squirrel scientist will come and help us see the inside of the dead squirrel—the muscles, heart, and stomach." The announcement generated great enthusiasm, and the visit was awaited with much anticipation. That Friday Judy was surrounded by children as she sat down to work. Unfortunately, I had taken the squirrel out of the freezer too late, and Judy was unable to work on the still-frozen specimen. The children were surprisingly accepting about the need to reschedule. Now that they had met Judy, the anticipation about her next visit was even greater.

Upon her second arrival in the preschool room, Judy drew a crowd. She and the entire class settled down around the long table, other popular activi-

Figure 1–3. *Jason's squirrel*

ties rejected in favor of watching the dead squirrel being opened. As she set up her equipment, Judy was bombarded with questions and comments. Lilly mentioned that she had "only seen the inside of an animal in a book." Jason was compelled to tell about a squirrel he saw outside "that was not dead." Aviva wanted to know what the scalpel was for. Jerry asked about the corn meal. "Judy, Judy, Judy" the group seemed to be calling in unison.

Judy handled these questions gracefully as she began the procedure. The first step was to use the scalpel to make a two-inch incision down the squirrel's belly. Judy then coated the inside of the skin with corn meal to provide friction, and used her fingers to separate the fur from the muscle. After a few minutes of hard work she had proceeded down from the midsection to the hind legs. After ten minutes Judy had freed the first leg. The children watched with rapt attention.

As she worked around the bottom of the carcass, Judy talked about the animal's bathrooming mechanism, a description the children thoroughly enjoyed. After twenty minutes, as Judy worked to free the second leg, Scott, Eduardo, and Jerry left to play with blocks. Finished with the hind legs and tail, Judy then worked back up toward the head. I had been monitoring Sean, warned by his parents that he might have trouble with the procedure. As Judy reached the head Sean began to look pale. I suggested he take a break from watching, an idea he gratefully accepted.

Nine children remained at the table (Jerry returned from the block area). I must admit to feeling a bit squeamish when Judy pulled the fur off the squirrel's head. This was an intimate experience. But the children were unfazed. When Judy asked if they thought the undertaking was hurting the squirrel Lilly responded matter of factly, "It's dead, so it can't get any deader."

The fur now off, Judy opened the body cavity. She showed the children the heart, lungs, and stomach. We learned the squirrel had died soon after eating a large meal. Judy then stuffed the fur with cotton, and sewed it up to make a scientific study skin for the class to keep. Through the hour-and-a-half operation children had come and gone as they wished. Lilly, Shoshana, Aviva, and Cleo sat transfixed through it all.

The next day Claude, Cleo's father, approached me. Since he only sought me out when there was a problem, usually about a misplaced article of clothing, I was apprehensive. "I have a question for you," he began. "Please, ask away," I responded, a smile hopefully concealing my nervousness. He continued:

*Claude:* Yesterday I noticed a lady here in the room.

*Ben:* Yes, that was Judy. I think I mentioned to you yesterday that Cleo was fascinated by her work with the squirrel. She must have sat and watched for an hour and a half.

*Claude:* Yes, yes, I know that. But don't you think. Well, I mean, I came in and saw that poor little squirrel lying there without its fur. Don't you think that it was a little too graphic for the children?

*Ben:* I thought about that beforehand. That's why watching the procedure was completely voluntary, and I kept an eye out to see if any of the children were disturbed. They were really intrigued by what was going on and fascinated when they saw the inside of the squirrel. The operation didn't seem to bother them.

Claude smiled, but then replied "Yes, yes, but what was the pedagogical point?"

I took a deep breath and collected my thoughts. I explained how interested preschoolers are in what is inside things: televisions, computers, and bodies. I mentioned how generally children only get to see the insides of bodies in books. I reiterated how captivated the children were by the experience.

What I didn't talk about, because I didn't think that Claude would understand, was that Judy's visit was much more than an informative anatomy lesson. The children and I had experienced something remarkable together. Embedded in a three-week unit, Judy's visit was the capstone of a compelling study which captivated the entire group. There was real engagement here. Through this engagement the child-teacher relationships that David Hawkins describes were forming. A community of learners was being created. That was the pedagogical point.

## The Slide Show

The squirrel unit concluded. Several months passed. We studied flags, boats, and then light. One day, in the midst of our astronomy unit, I told the children I had a surprise for them.

The surprise was a slide show composed of shots taken during the squirrel unit. When the first slides appeared on the screen the children shouted excitedly, "That's me" as they recognized themselves. They laughed when I reminded them that during the slide of the group playing their harmonicas, they were jamming along with the Squirrel Nut Zippers. "That's Judy!" they called out when the series of dissection slides appeared.

I had two reactions watching the slide show. First, nostalgia. Though only a few months had passed, it was clear to me that much ground had been travelled by the children and myself. These slides showed the beginning of a journey. The children watching the slides were my students. The children in the slides were just becoming my students. While I had no desire to return to this early stage of our relationship, just as I have no desire for my sons to be infants again, I was touched by the memories of my initial days with this group.

I was also impressed by what the children remembered about the squirrel unit. Jerry, Pierce, Cleo, and Jessie recognized pictures they had drawn of the dead squirrel. Jerry and Aviva recognized Zealand's page from the *Silly Squirrel Book*. Shoshana recalled that we had seen lots of gray squirrels, some chipmunks, but no red squirrels. And Pierce remembered the final census total: one hundred and eleven.

## In the Beginning . . .

Studying squirrels was a beginning. Over the course of the year this group of children and I explored topics ranging from astronomy to South Africa, and basketball to the Beatles. When I describe these later curriculum units to fellow teachers a common reaction is, "That's wonderful, but it couldn't happen in my classroom." A teacher told me that my curriculum was possible because I was working with "future Nobel Prize winners," forwarding the notion that average preschoolers could not engage in such topics.

The majority of children I work with have highly educated parents, and it is certainly true that working with children whose families value what I do with curriculum makes my job easier. But I also like to think that the way in which Cathy and I organize our classroom plays a role here; that by presenting compelling units the children become invested in studying. My sense is that the children learn from the beginning that what goes on in the preschool room is exciting, challenging, and fun. When I tell my students we will be studying the Beatles next, their reaction is, "Let's go!" even if their next comment is, "What's a beatle?"

My experience with preschoolers is, no matter what their background, when they are presented compelling curriculum their reaction is, "Let's go!" The comments of the astute observer of childhood, Erik Erikson (1950), confirm my impressions. Erikson wrote of the preschool years that, "The child is at no time more ready to learn . . . [and] profit from teachers" (258). Preschoolers are full of energy and initiative. They are ready to work together and learn. They are hungry for compelling curriculum.

Cleo, the youngster whose father was unclear about the pedagogical point of observing the dead squirrel, is in this way a wonderful example of preschoolhood. Fresh off the plane from France at the beginning of the school year, Cleo spoke no English. Included in Cleo's first hundred English words were "squirrel" and "acorn." By the time her English vocabulary had doubled, included was the word "study."

## Resources

The members of the *Sciuridae* family can be found almost anywhere. *Sciurus carolinesis,* the familiar gray squirrel with its long, bushy tail, ranges from Quebec south to Florida, and west to Texas. Introduced to the Pacific coast, gray squirrels are also found in Washington State and British Columbia. Adaptable to human environs and not timid around people, these squirrels are easily observed in urban, suburban, and rural settings. *Tamiasciurus hudsonicus,* the red squirrel, is transcontinental, ranging from Quebec south to the Carolinas, and west to California. These squirrels make their homes in conifer stands and are seen mainly in forested areas. *Glaucomys volans,* the fascinating flying squirrel, is found throughout North America, from Southern Ontario to the Gulf Coast and west to California and Mexico. They are reputably as numerous as gray squirrels. However, their nocturnal habits and shy disposition make sightings rare (although Jerry claims to have seen one in flight over the day care parking lot). From the mouse-sized pygmy squirrels of Central Africa to the four-foot-long (nose to tail) giant flying squirrels of Borneo, there are over two hundred squirrel species worldwide. As any squirrel scientist can tell you, only Madagascar and Australia are lacking for squirrels.

Such detailed information about squirrels can be gathered from many guide and reference books. *Wild Mammals of New England* by Alfred Godin (Baltimore: Johns Hopkins Press, 1977) offers descriptions of gray, red, and flying squirrels. For Internet users, a number of squirrel websites are located at http://members.aol.com/sqrillovers/links.htm. Among the resources available here are links to rehabilitators for help with injured or orphaned squirrels, images of squirrels, and a fascinating description by the staff of the Brookside Nature Center in Wheaton, Maryland, on their efforts studying the elusive, beguiling southern flying squirrel. You don't have to be an AOL member to visit these sites.

For the preschool crowd, my list of favorite books about squirrels includes Lois Ehlert's *Nuts to You!* (San Diego: Harcourt, Brace, Jovanovich, 1993). Ehlert combines paper-cut illustrations with a fun-filled story about an uninvited squirrel visitor to introduce readers to the habits of city-dwelling gray squirrels. Brian Wildsmith's *Squirrels* (New York: Scholastic, 1974), with its attractive watercolor paintings and interesting list of facts is also a good introduction to the gray squirrel. With photographs of squirrels hunting for seeds and avoiding predators, *Gray Squirrel at Pacific Avenue* by Geri Harrington (Norwalk, CT: Trudy, 1995) rounds out the *Sciurus carolinesis* reading list. *The Raggedy Red Squirrel* by Hope Ryden (New York: Dutton, 1992) weaves great photographs and a simple text to tell about the gray squirrel's smaller, pinenut-eating cousin. Captivating photographs of baby red squirrels and flying squirrels are found in *Rabbits and Other Small Mammals* by Don Earnest and Richard Oulahan (New York: Time Life, 1978).

The Squirrel Nut Zippers, with their blend of jazz, ragtime, and bayou swing, are available on Mammoth Records (based in Carrboro, North Carolina). The children's favorite tune, "Keep the Lid on It," is the second cut on their CD *Hot.*

Cousin Seth's famous acorn muffin recipe is as follows: Gather approximately 50 white oak acorns. *Be sure to use acorns from white oak trees,* identified by the rounded lobes of their leaves. Shell and then boil the meat to draw out the tannic acid. Discard the red liquid and reboil several times. Place the acorns on a baking sheet, and set them in the oven for 1 hour at a low temperature to dry. Grind the dried acorns into flour using a mill or food processor. The results should be approximately 1 cup of acorn flour. Mix the acorn flour with 1 cup of wheat flour. Add 3 tsps. baking powder, 1 tsp. salt, and 3 Tbsps. sugar. In a separate bowl, mix together 3 Tbsps. melted butter, 2 egg yolks, and 1½ cups of buttermilk. Mix the dry and wet ingredients. Fold in 2 stiffly beaten egg whites. Bake in greased muffin tins for 20–25 minutes at 375°F. Bon appetit.

My thanks to Dr. Gary Alpert for his prompt and enthusiastic response to my questions about the dead squirrel, and for getting me in touch with Judy Chupasko. Many thanks to Judy for generously giving her time to provide my class with a view of squirrels that few preschoolers, let alone adults, get to experience.

# 2

## Reaching for the Stars: Astronomy

## The Wonders of Orion

As a boy I was fascinated with space. My bedroom door was plastered with newspaper clippings about the Gemini program, my most prized possession a telescope purchased with money saved from a paper route, and my play filled with fantasies of rocket travel. Favorite destinations included Jupiter's giant red spot and our moon's Sea of Tranquility. As I grew older, these extraterrestrial interests were gradually replaced by more down-to-earth concerns.

My fascination with space was rekindled several years ago when, walking down a country road one crystal clear night, I was treated to a dazzling performance of seemingly countless stars glistening overhead. It was as if the sky was talking, even singing, as expressed in a Native American poem I later came across:

> We are the stars which sing,
> We sing with our light.
> We are the birds of fire,
> We fly over the sky.
> Our light is a voice.
> We make a road,
> For the spirit to pass over.

With renewed interest in astronomy, I dusted off my childhood telescope, obtained a field guide to the night sky, and began an exploration of the heavens.

In the city where I live, the night sky is not as dramatic as out in the country. The glare of street lights substantially reduces the number of visible stars. Still, points of interest remain, among them the clearly discernible and easily recognized stars of the constellation Orion.

I began my exploration of the heavens with Orion because it is so easy to identify. The row of three bright stars that make up Orion's belt are unlike anything else in the sky. Not surprisingly, virtually every culture tells a story about this prominent group of stars. To the ancient Egyptians, these stars were the resting place of Osiris, the god of the underworld and of creativity, who murdered his brother Set. In Indian mythology, they represent Projapati, lord of all creatures, who fathered twenty-seven daughters. To medieval Arab astronomers the stars were Al Jabar, The Giant.

The Western European story of Orion originated in Greek mythology. A great but boastful hunter, Orion earned the animus of the spiteful goddess Hera. To vent her wrath, she sent a scorpion to Orion's bedside to kill the hunter. Orion awoke at the scorpion's deadly sting and smashed the arachnid with his club before succumbing to its poison. According to legend, this is why Orion and the scorpion are never seen together—Orion a winter constellation, and Scorpius part of the summer sky.

As I've gotten to know the individual members of Orion my appreciation of the constellation has grown. The prominent star to the northeast of the belt is Betelgeuse. Arabic for "the armpit of the giant," Betelgeuse is the eleventh brightest star in the sky. Its massive circumference is as large as the earth's entire orbit and its red-orangish tint evidence that this ancient star is in a final stage of stellar evolution.

On the opposite side of the belt is Rigel, the seventh brightest star in the sky. Rigel's intense bluish hue contrasts its neighbor's reddish coloration and is indicative of a very hot, relatively young star. A supergiant, Rigel is 50,000 times more luminous than our sun. It would be more accurate to call this object Rigels, for high-powered instruments reveal this point of light to be actually two stars that orbit each other. Such binary systems are common in our galaxy.

Observing Betelgeuse, Rigel, and the other stars of Orion, we are actually looking back in time. For example, Mintaka, the most westerly of the belt stars, is 1,500 light years away from the earth. That means that it takes 1,500 years for light to travel between Mintaka and our solar system. Looking at Mintaka you are not observing it as it appears today, but as it looked in the year 499. And we won't be getting any more current with this star. Mintaka is moving away from the earth at a rate of 12.5 miles per second. That's 450,000 miles per hour on a car speedometer, swift to us mortals, but a mere pittance when compared to the mind boggling 670,515,200 miles per hour at which light travels.

The more I learn about this corner of the sky with its scores of stars and nebulae the more I come to appreciate its complexity and subtlety. Learning about Orion is a bit like getting to know your neighbor. You wave to the old man across the street; you arrive home at night and gaze up at Rigel. Both create familiar and satisfying feelings. But there's more to them than that. Learning about Betelgeuse's color and its age has transformed this star from an anonymous point of light to an entryway into the vastness of the universe. Looking at Mintaka and knowing that it is 1,500 light years away, momentarily transports me above and beyond the mundane concerns of daily life. Like knowing the robin's call or being able to identify a Lady Slipper in the woods, knowing Rigel's name connects me with what are, for all practical purposes, infinite and eternal aspects of our universe that are apart from the often flawed nature of human existence. My imagination soars as I look up at Orion, wondering about what lies beyond our little planet.

## Why Astronomy?

Celestial rhetoric aside, the question, Why study astronomy with young children? remains. I'll concede from the outset that *my* interest in astronomy was the primary motivation for studying the sky. I believe that when teachers bring their interests into the classroom, they convey a genuine enthusiasm and sense of wonder for the topic. This enthusiasm can turn ordinary activities into compelling curriculum if the children also become excited about the topic of study. I had a high degree of confidence that this would be the case with astronomy; that what I found fascinating about the sky—the stories, the information, and the simple beauty—would also command the children's attention.

Further, I wanted to introduce the children to the job of astronomer. While not as famous among the four-year-old set as firefighters, mechanics, or ballerinas, astronomers are also involved in exciting, important work. They make careful observations, record data, theorize about phenomena, and discuss with colleagues ways to prove or improve their ideas—activities I wanted my charges to engage in. I also hoped that familiarity with astronomers and astronomy would translate into a comfort with scientists and science, that the children would regard science as something that was accessible to them.

Finally, studying astronomy seemed like a good way to counter what I find to be the most depressing aspect of winter: darkness. In January where I live it is dark by 4:30. The children do not respond well to this either. For them darkness means it is time to be home. Unfortunately, there is still an hour left in the day, and they grow impatient for their parents' arrivals. My grandfather, a man brimming with folk wisdom and common sense, was fond of telling me to turn problems into perks. Using his advice, I turned the darkness to our advantage by studying it.

What follows is a description of my class' month-long exploration of space. Embedded in the essay are thoughts demonstrating:

- how observations of children can guide curriculum;
- how stories can bring a topic of study to life; and
- how tapping into children's fantasy and play can advance inquiry.

Interestingly, stories, fantasy, and play take on particular importance when the subject matter is something children cannot touch, like astronomy.

## Preschool Astronomers

Space is a very big place. In our tiny corner of the universe alone, the solar system contains nine planets, scores of moons, comets, asteroids, and one average-sized star. Beyond our immediate neighborhood there are innumerable stars, nebulae, quasars, black holes, galaxies, and objects yet to be discovered or named. Space is literally an infinite topic.

The task of teaching preschoolers about such a huge subject was daunting, and required some thought. As I brainstormed how to present astronomy to my class, I made two important decisions. The first was to divide the unit into three sections: the planets, the moon, and the stars (including our sun). This division was not meant as a rigid order, but rather as a guide that would provide coherence to my presentation of materials.

The second decision was more far-reaching: to wrap the study of astronomy in story and play. This was a critical decision. The infusion of drama can help bring a topic of study to life for any age group. For young children, who frequently use play as a means for exploring the world, including drama in their studies can prove invaluable. Years of teaching young children has convinced me of the truism of the paradox that delving into fantasy makes the study of reality more accessible, and real to children. To this end, I wanted my class to take on the personae of astronomers to facilitate their exploration of the sky.

If the children were to learn about the heavens by playing astronomer, they would need props. The most important prop would be the astronomer's workplace, so I set about finding a suitable site for an observatory. Because of its sense of separateness and its visual access to the sky, I selected the loft, a seven-by-seven foot crow's nest with an exterior window. In order to make the necessary preparations and build suspense about the upcoming unit of study, I closed the loft the week preceding our astronomy unit. Counting down the days until they again could use the loft the children became increasingly excited about studying space.

I furnished our observatory with the essentials for preschool astronomers: work stations consisting of tables, chairs, and computer keyboards; markers, pencils, rulers, and paper for making observations; and, of course, telescopes, made of cardboard tubes and facing out the window, for viewing celestial objects. To enhance the astronomical mood I taped up photographs of the moon, planets, and asteroids along with pictures of real-life astronomers at work.

Amid much fanfare "The Flying Castle," the name the children voted to give the observatory, was opened. Having waited an entire week for the opportunity, children flocked to the loft, drawing, computing, and using the telescopes. Physicist Chet Raymo has written that looking through a telescope is 50 percent observation and 50 percent imagination. In this case it was 100 percent imagination, but with their imaginations the children were seeing a great deal: Mars, Venus, an asteroid or two, and even previously undiscovered planets.

Everyone, that is, with the exception of James. The opening of the observatory coincided with James' first day in the preschool room. Fresh off an airplane from England, James was mystified by his new classmates' ability to see planets through cardboard tubes, insisting that for the observatory to be "real" it required authentic instruments. Perhaps James was unfamiliar with fantasy play receiving such overt teacher sanction, or perhaps his insistence on a strict adherence to reality was part of his adjustment to a new setting. Whatever the cause, the issue was soon moot. By the second day James had learned how to use the telescopes, and his drawings of planets and asteroids took their place on the observatory walls alongside those of the other children.

## The Planets (and Asteroids!)

James and his classmates had effortlessly taken on the personae of astronomers. Now they were ready to go to work. Work for these children meant sociodramatic play, group improvisations of scenes created out of the children's collective striving to make sense of their world. Dramatic play is a ubiquitous phenomenon in preschool classrooms, with children's imaginations leading them to become mothers, fathers, babies, and superheroes out in the play yard, in the house corner, in the block area, and even at the snack table. My hope was that the role of astronomer would become coveted in the children's play.

To promote celestial play, I provided the children with compelling materials about space, including factual information about the planets and stars, stories about astronomers at work, songs about the heavens, and even tastes of the food eaten aboard the space shuttles. Following my organizational plan for dividing space into manageable subtopics, the first materials provided to the newly minted astronomers focused on the planets.

Books were a ready source of planetary material. I filled our bookshelves with volumes about the solar system. Books providing breathtaking images of our eight neighbors and their satellites furnished the children's imaginations with concrete images to draw upon as they undertook their astronomical play. The books also contained interesting facts, which the children used to spice up their drama. References to facts lent an air of authenticity to the children's fantasies.

Stories, because of their close relationship to play, were another natural planetary material. I told the class a dozen tales about the planets. Each was infused with an enthusiasm about astronomy, information about the solar system, and readymade scripts for dramatic play. Witness the weeklong epic about how the children took a trip through the solar system, the first astronomers to undertake such a journey. I began the story's first installment by describing the boarding of a spacecraft. Props procured from the block area, and representing the spaceship and each preschool astronomer aided the enactment of the journey's onset. As the rocket sped away from the earth into deep space, I turned on a recording of Gustav Holst's "The Planets." The eerie sounds created by the orchestra provided a perfect backdrop for revealing the mission's first destination: Mars. I intoned:

> For the past one hundred years astronomers have debated about the existence of life on Mars. Some astronomers, peering through their telescopes, claimed to see canals crisscrossing the planet, evidence of intelligent life. Other astronomers scoffed at such notions, arguing that Mars is far too cold to support life. Recently, an asteroid from Mars was found near the South Pole. The asteroid had tiny specks which some geologists feel are fossils of germs. If this is true, then there very well may be life on Mars. But no one knows for sure, because no one has ever visited Mars. Until now. The preschool astronomers can help solve this mystery. The first stop of our mission is the red planet to investigate the question: *Is there life on Mars?*

After landing, the explorers had an exciting excursion on the planet's surface. They traveled across a reddish plain, photographed the enormous volcano Olympus Mons, and collected soil samples. But then, out of nowhere, a sandstorm erupted, forcing the astronomers back to their ship. To avoid damage by the characteristically strong Martian winds, the preschoolers quickly left for their next destination. The question of life on Mars was left unresolved.

My choice of block props for the solar system saga was a considered attempt to inspire space play. I hoped that the children would embark on missions of their own in the block area. Efforts at having adult stories directly influence children's play are a bit like going fishing, with luck as well as skill determining the results. In this case I was lucky. Over the next few days the block area saw a great deal of astronomy play. Rocketships were built, launched, and then piloted by the preschool astronomers to distant planets. Often these missions involved the search for extraterrestrial life.

Next door, in the loft, significant work was also taking place. There were the discoveries that Neptune consisted mainly of ice cream, and that Pluto was made of candy. More reality-based were sightings of Saturn's rings, and of "a new planet four times the size of Jupiter near Pegasus 51." But the most exciting observations were of the approaching asteroids.

James was the first to spot the asteroids. After looking through the telescopes, he announced:

> We saw a very big space rock that's going to crash into Mars. If it crashes into Mars, Mars is going to break into pieces and fall on Earth. We've got to control it.

James' report was updated by Michael's account that, while providing a temporary reprieve from the space rocks (now called asteroids), hinted at future disaster:

> An asteroid is going to go from here to there to there and then it's going to hit the little planet. We have to stop it. We saved the day! Instead of going into Pluto we headed it into the sun. *But there's another one out there.*

Over the next few days, as Max, Janet, Maddy, Joy, Michael, Michele, James, and Jack worked up in the observatory, there were numerous bulletins about the asteroids. My favorite was a report from Jack. Brief and to the point, Jack explained:

> Asteroid hits. All dead. Bad luck.

My role in this high-energy play, beyond policing the occasional breach of classroom decorum, was predicated on listening. By listening to the children's play I was able to utilize my own knowledge base and experience to offer occasional suggestions that could extend and enrich the drama. This included astronomical vocabulary—for example, that space rocks could be called asteroids. This also meant forwarding possible dramatic twists. Because of the block area's proximity to the observatory, I encouraged the astronomers in each area to send one another reports. Collaboration followed, as in the following discussion between James (in the block area) and Jack (in the observatory) regarding those pesky asteroids:

*James:* Press the button with the arrow going up. It's the only way to save us.

*Jack:* I got it. I did it. I saved our lives!

Despite this success, communications between the two areas were not always effective. The block area's spaceships were often damaged and even destroyed by asteroids. When such disasters occurred, I suggested that the astronomers collect some of the fallen asteroids and make block microscopes to analyze the rocks from space. Through such analysis the preschool astronomers discovered that asteroids consist of "rock, ice, and chicken bones."

Listening also meant that I was an attentive audience for these budding astronomers. In that role I was told a great deal, the children anxious to explain their endeavors and discoveries. A benefit of listening to the children's reports was learning what most interested my charges about astronomy. What I learned will come as no surprise; asteroids were very compelling. It was not coincidental that in my ongoing tale of the preschooler astronomers' travels through the solar system I related an installment featuring close encounters with asteroids. The cross-pollinization of the children's and my stories enriched the narratives of all involved.

A week had gone by, and the reviews of the astronomy unit were generally favorable. A majority of the class was into it, some *very* into it. Children talked about their favorite planets—a sure sign of interest. Walks to the park spontaneously became trips into space, with clouds seen as Venus' poisonous gases and unexpected gusts signalling the beginnings of Martian sandstorms.

But interest in astronomy was uneven. Kim, Robert, Joseph, and Katie, the youngest children in the group, often did not connect to the curriculum. My observations suggested this pattern was continuing with astronomy. Their play seemed unaffected by the unit of study. There was no hint of planets in their art work or stories. Their visits to the observatory were short and uneventful. When I asked little Katie what we were studying, she responded, "Studying?"

## The Race to the Moon

While noteworthy, my observations of Kim, Robert, Joseph, and Katie were not cause for panic. Given their age, and that they had only been preschoolers a few months, it was not out of the ordinary that they had yet to become part of the community of learners their classmates subscribed to. That said, January is the time I look for all the children to become part of our community. It was a major goal of the month to hook the four on curriculum.

To understand why Kim, Robert, Joseph, and Katie had yet to connect with the curriculum and plan out strategies to bring them into the class' orbit, I went over the anecdotal notes I try to take during the course of each day. These notes are the product of my walking around the classroom with a pen and note card, jotting down events of interest, such as peer interactions, exploration time choices, and conversations. I turn these scribbles into comprehensible commentary once at home. I also recalled conversations with parents and discussed each child extensively with Cathy.

My observations of Kim suggested he was a candidate to become heavily involved in curriculum. Friendly, bright, and enthusiastic, Kim was clearly interested in the world around him. He made insightful observations on our walks and enjoyed the puppet stories and folk tales I told. But he was also fixated on Power Rangers (the superheroes du jour), an interest he shared with his best friend Robert. Ranger play was a major pillar of this relationship, and the two spent hours acting out the aggressive play scenarios they had seen on TV. In fact, Kim seemed to think the primary reason for the day care center's existence was to provide a venue for him to play Power Rangers with Robert. Activities that hindered this goal—nap, meetings—were endured out of obligation. Activities that facilitated this goal—outside play, exploration time—were relished. Because of his social orientation, the key to involving Kim in curriculum was getting Robert involved.

Robert was a thoughtful, gentle boy. We had a good relationship, with Robert initiating conversations and making me presents of his drawings—generally red, green and yellow blotches representing different Power Rangers. Robert's limited vocabulary indicated delays in his expressive language. Because he often seemed not to understand directions, and because his mind wandered during the language-based meeting times, Cathy and I suspected there were delays in his receptive language as well. This did not limit his enjoyment of dramatic play, however. Robert had a rich fantasy life and was often someone or something other than Robert. Play that did not require sophisticated language was the clear venue for him to engage in the curriculum.

Joseph and Katie's place in the room was complicated by a common fate: both children's parents were splitting up. As a result, they had a lot more to think about besides astronomy. The two reacted to their families' turmoil in very different ways. Joseph became mulish, trying to retain control over a world that was spinning out of control. He resisted anything that he sensed adults wanted him to do. This was most clearly manifested in his stubborn refusal to toilet train. At the same time, his needs made him very vulnerable, and he relied a great deal on the emotional support (verbal comforting, sitting on laps) he received from Cathy and me. A very bright child, he spent much time talking about "The Nutcracker," though when we later studied dance he deftly avoided participating in the ballet. Astronomy, because of its association with adults, was suspect.

Katie employed a different defense mechanism, trying her best to ignore reality. At meeting times she seemed preoccupied. At exploration times she wandered around the classroom, having difficulty engaging. She was never disruptive, but her mind was clearly elsewhere. Katie had some important friendships, and enjoyed painting and drawing, but she had yet to grasp that the preschoolers were involved in curriculum.

While I wanted to engage Joseph and Katie in curriculum, my foremost goal was to provide the two with a safe, secure place to be. I offered my lap for comfort, worked hard on building relationships, and practiced patience when it came to curriculum. I hoped that when they saw their peers' excitement about studying, they might give the curriculum a try.

During the second week of the astronomy unit I began introducing material about the moon. As we switched attention to our nearest celestial neighbor, I was determined to address the nonparticipation of my four youngest students. The strategy was simple: employ action-oriented dramatic play. With them in mind, Cathy and I refurnished the block area. Cathy obtained a child-sized box which we dubbed "the Mercury orbiter." I brought over chairs, helmets, and large plastic "waffle" blocks (foot-square interlocking plastic components) from which the children could fashion a larger space craft.

These materials were intended to say "rocketship." However, I knew better than to assume the children would dutifully adopt our vision for the block area. I was particularly leery of Kim and Robert who, left to their own devices, would almost certainly have turned the block area into a staging ground for Power Ranger play. Of course, I would have stopped such play, but at the cost of further distancing the two from the classroom curriculum. To avoid such a scenario, it was necessary to promote exciting alternatives for play on the block area stage.

Alternatives were provided in "The Race to the Moon," a story I told the children over the course of the week. The story began:

> Isn't the moon amazing, how it rises in the sky, sometimes a huge ball, at other times a tiny sliver. Throughout history people have been fascinated by the moon, and dreamed of traveling to it. Not long before I was born, rockets were invented. For the first time there was a real chance to travel to the moon. Astronomers were thrilled about the possibility of going to the moon and studying it.

To build suspense, I then introduced the central dramatic tension of the story:

> Forty years ago, when astronomers realized that people might actually be able to travel to the moon, there were two countries that were always hav-

ing contests: our own country, the United States, and the Soviet Union. The leaders of these two countries decided that getting to the moon first would be another contest. *The race to the moon was on!*

While I was ambivalent about such a jingoistic story line, even in the relatively benign topic of space exploration, I knew framing the story as a race would have great appeal. I was right, and the children were instantly hooked by the story.

The story's first installment concluded with descriptions of Russia's early successes in space, and America's initial failures. The children loved my slapstick presentation of how the first American rockets went up, and then very quickly came down (or went sideways, or turned upside down). Later installments of "The Race to the Moon" featured the Mercury Missions and Alan Shepard, Apollo 8's trip to and around (but not on) the moon, and finally Apollo 11, Neil Armstrong, and "One small step for man, one giant leap for mankind." Details about space exploration that could easily be incorporated into the children's play, such as preparations for liftoff, countdowns, and moonwalks were liberally sprinkled into the story.

The story's final episode helped allay my guilt about framing the narrative as a competition. I told the children how the former adversaries in the race to the moon were now cooperating in space. Coincidentally, that very week a U.S. space shuttle docked with the Russian space station Mir (the Russian word for peace).

My efforts at providing alternative play scenarios were handsomely rewarded. Kim, Robert, and even Joseph became very interested in making spaceships. They had countdowns, flew off to the moon, and fashioned air tanks out of paper-towel tubes to help them on their moonwalks. Their interest in space spilled over to other parts of the day, and they paid closer attention to meeting time activities, visited the observatory, and joined their peers in drawing space objects. Other children were also involved in the space missions, and the block area was filled with talk about Alan Shepard, Apollo 8, and solemn pronouncements like, "One small step for man." Only Katie remained aloof. My hope was that other activities, other entry points, would pull her into the curriculum.

Some of these other entry points came at meeting times. As a group we orbited and rotated, boogied to Van Morrison's "Moondance," and sang folk guitarist Greg Brown's tune "Rooty Toot Toot for the Moon." The song's speculation that the moon is a "slice of green cheese" segued neatly into discussing the moon's composition.

Another activity that fired the children's interest was seeing the moon. On the first walk of the week I challenged the children to find the moon in the sky. Its discovery brought much excitement. On subsequent walks the children undertook the lunar search without prompting. On our return to the center we dutifully recorded what the moon looked like as it waxed toward full.

At the end of the week I arranged a trip to a local observatory. The visit was intended to enrich the children's play by allowing them to see a real astronomer's workplace. Much to my disappointment, bad weather forced the cancellation of our trip. Fortunately, we were able to shift gears and visit Boston's Museum of Science. There, the entire group piled into an Apollo Orbiter, excitedly counting down for an imaginary trip to the moon. Upon splash down, we made our way to the planetarium.

To planetarium or not to planetarium; that is the question teachers studying astronomy must confront. My recommendation? A qualified yes. Why? My group had a wonderful experience. The presentation was geared to young children, and the visual images were simply incredible. Kim and Robert, my TV junkies, were particularly taken with the show. Without a doubt, everyone left the museum more excited about astronomy. So why the qualification? Trips to the planetarium are expensive. There is also the real worry that the planetarium's large, dark space might terrify some children.

Overall, interest in astronomy grew during our study of the moon. The observatory continued to be a popular destination, with the addition of a digital clock providing another level to observations. Children recorded the time their pictures were drawn, making series of observations. Lunar art activities were also popular, with children cutting different moon shapes to represent the lunar phases. Most telling were parental reports that astronomy was coming home. Maddy's mother recounted how her daughter, staring out the car window at the moon, muttered incredulously, "They stuck a flag up there."

## Stars and Stories

During the third and fourth weeks of the astronomy curriculum I presented material about the stars, including our own sun, through story and play while also providing opportunities to sing about, paint, and discuss the stars.

In preparation for our visit to the observatory the children generated a list of questions for the resident astronomer. Their questions included:

- What are the stars and moon made of?
- How were the stars, moon, and planets born?
- How big is the solar system?
- How big is the entire universe?

The cancellation of the observatory trip left these questions unanswered. With the shift of focus from the moon to the stars, it seemed like an appropriate time to address some of the children's big questions about space.

The meeting time discussions that followed were too abstract for some children, but for those who did participate, the discussions were heady experiences involving a high level of theorizing and debating. The discussion about how the stars and moon were created is a case in point, and is a good example of how teacher-structured conversations can help stretch children's thinking.

I began the discussion by inviting the children to assume their astronomer personas; to address the issue "like astronomers do; to think together to try to answer hard questions." Inspired, Maddy bravely entered the fray, putting forth an idea. After I questioned her, she refined her hypothesis to say, "The moon came from the sun and the moon made the stars." Our discussion was launched.

Astronomer Jack was skeptical about the idea that the moon came from the sun:

*Jack:* I don't agree because how could that happen because the moon is made of rock and the sun is made of burning gas; it's so hot it's fire. How could rock come from fire?

Jack's critique deeply offended Maddy, and left the other children silent. Feeling action was needed to keep the discussion from crash-landing, I ventured:

*Ben:* That's what a lot of astronomers are trying to figure out. If you have all this hot gas how do you get stone? But what if the sun let some gas out and it cooled down?

*Max:* Lava could do that.

*Ben:* So maybe there is something to Maddy's idea.

James, who was anxiously awaiting an opportunity to speak, then addressed the portion of the hypothesis that the stars came from the moon:

*James:* Maybe asteroids picked up parts of the moon and that made the craters, and then dropped off the stars and that's what made the stars.

*Ben:* What do you think about James' idea?

*Max:* I know craters came from asteroids.

*Ben:* What about asteroids picking up the stars?

*Jack:* I agree with that too.

*Max:* But how can stars come from stone?

*Jack:* The stars are stone.

*Max:* No they aren't. They're fire.

Jack and Max's dispute led our conversation into a debate about the composition of the stars. Eventually, I brought the discussion to a close by concluding, "you are just like real astronomers: presenting ideas, disagreeing, and making your ideas better."

Our cosmological discussions did not produce any scientific breakthroughs, nor did they necessarily lead children to a more accurate understanding of the genesis of the stars, planets, and moon. They weren't meant to. I helped structure these conversations so the children could get a taste of scientific discourse. Rather than encumber the discussions with facts beyond the children's grasp, I elected to allow the children to consider possibilities like asteroids picking up stars from the moon. The result was lively, free-ranging conversations in which children felt like astronomers.

Not all our explorations of the stars were language-based. The stars also inspired a new series of art projects, the most interesting inspired by the children viewing Vincent Van Gogh's "Starry Night." Holding a reprint of the painting, I told the children it was one artist's way of portraying the night sky.

Provided with the blue, white, yellow, brown, green, and black paint found in the original, the children then enthusiastically got to work making their own representations. The results were predictably varied. Some children incorporated Van Gogh's ideas in their work. James' paper was filled with yellow dots on the top, and a large cone-shaped object rising from the bottom. He informed me that the original painting gave him, "The good idea to make these stars, and the tall green thing gave me the idea to make Everest." Max's effort was more closely modeled on Van Gogh. He filled the top of his painting with a swirling blue background dotted with yellow stars and a crescent moon. The bottom was covered with green trees next to a cluster of houses. But Max, who was not striving for an exact replica, also requested red paint so he could include Mars and Betelgeuse in his work (Figure 2–1).

Michele and Katie collaborated, eventually layering on so much paint that it wasn't clear what was being represented. Robert, who had fallen in love with Venus, only had eyes for that planet when he painted a swirling round, bluish object for his night sky.

In our study of the stars we of course took advantage of the late afternoon darkness. One evening we bundled up, went outside, spotted some stars, and chanted the familiar poem, "Star light, star bright, first star we see tonight . . ." After making wishes we adjourned inside to drink hot chocolate. The next day I told the children we were going out to see another star—in broad daylight. Amid grumbling that, "You can't see stars during the day," we trudged outside to a suitable viewpoint. Perched on a westward-looking vista bathed in sunlight we talked about our nearest star, the sun—why it seemed so much bigger than the stars we had seen the night before, and why the sunlight felt warm on our faces. We then enjoyed a beautiful sunset.

Figure 2–1. *Child's take on Van Gogh's* Starry Night

## Star Stories

The most compelling entry points into the universe beyond our solar system were star stories; narratives whose inspiration came from the stars. The sky is a veritable treasure chest of stories. Tales about the constellations and individual stars abound throughout history. The early astronomers were astrologers as well. Even in contemporary astronomy, the constellations play an important role. The International Astronomical Union divides the sky into eighty-eight regions or constellations. Familiarity with these constellations is essential to knowing one's way around the sky. For children studying the stars, stories help increase awareness and promote interest in the variety and individuality of these shimmering lights in the night sky.

That said, I must admit that until fairly recently I had little interest in star stories. I could never see what I was "supposed to" in the sky, and felt alienated from constellation-based tales. A visit to the Hayden Planetarium in Boston changed this. As part of a program entitled "The Night Sky," the astronomer on duty, Ron Dandowitz, was giving the usual tour de force of the heavens. When he came to Pegasus he explained that the ancients saw a winged horse among this group of stars, and asked rhetorically, "Now don't you see that too?" I didn't, and was feeling a bit depressed about my lack of imagination when Ron intoned over the PA system, "Neither do I." As he moved an arrow around the great square of Pegasus, he explained, "When I look at these stars I see Fenway Park. Here is first base, second base, third base, and home plate." As the audience laughed in appreciation, I realized that I no longer needed to strain to imagine the constellations as they are portrayed in some medieval depiction of the sky, but was free to let my mind create its own imagery. This is not to say the Greek, Hindi, and Native American myths can't inspire contemporary storytellers, but that there are countless ways to look at the stars. The most meaningful stories are those that emerge from one's own imagination.

During the two weeks we focused on the stars I told a dozen star stories. I began each session by showing the children a chart of the featured constellation. These charts showed the relative magnitudes of each star along with the deep space objects located in the region. Asking the children what they noticed about these charts led to discussions of double stars, variable stars, red giants, super novas, nebulae, and galaxies.

The stories followed. Some of my tales had their starting points in the ancient myths, though they were never verbatim retellings. For example, my human female characters tended to be more assertive than the damsels in distress in the originals. Andromeda, who in Greek mythology waited helplessly for Perseus to save her from the monster Centus, vanquished the horrid sea creature herself in my version. In doing so she earned the title, "The Princess with the Sword." In other stories I completely dispensed with tradition. For example, the day my car broke down on the way to work, the constellation Hercules became "The Mechanic from the Sky," a magical person who came from the heavens in a AAA truck and instantly repaired my starter. The children eagerly awaited these stories, sitting mesmerized during the tellings.

Naturally, I provided the children with the means to create their own star stories. Supplied with glue, sequins, and markers, they quickly got to work creating products that were as fascinating as they were varied. Some children stuck to reality, producing models of the Big Dipper and Orion. Others worked in the realm of complete fantasy, creating new groups of stars such as Jack's "The Constellation Thorny Bush." But what was truly remarkable was how the children, like the ancients, projected their hopes and fears onto the night sky.

Joy, who lives with her mother and sister, and who has never met her father, dictated companion star stories to me on consecutive days. Entitled "Mommy" and "Dadda," both tales involved a nuclear family of two sisters, a mother, and the missing father. "Mommy," a rosy, benign tale, told of the two girls growing up from babyhood to preschoolhood. "Dadda" began in a similar vein, but soon took a dark turn. Unable to sustain the myth of the good father, Joy described how a monster devoured the two sisters as their inattentive father slept.

Michael, wrestling with issues of growing up and identification with male role models, told a tale entitled "The Knight." Covering some strongly archetypal terrain, the story began:

Once upon a time there was a knight. A boy was fighting the knight. The boy wanted to be like his father. The boy broke his promise—isn't that bad—and became evil with the help of the dragon.

James, who was new to the classroom, told a metaphorical tale of his experiences trying to enter this tight-knit group of children, a process complicated by his occasional habit of hitting to express himself. After hearing about the Pleiades, a cluster of stars located in Taurus, James (who in his dramatic play often pretended to be an asteroid) told a story entitled "The Star Meeting":

All the stars gathered together. Very close together. They talked about the sun. And they talked about the moon and the earth. But earth came to the meeting as well. And also the moon. They talked about the other galaxies that they'd seen. They talked about asteroids that sometimes hit them.

These stories literally poured out of the children. Through such telling the children created their own mythology of the sky, and began to take hold of the world above. This process has been described by the poet Rainer Maria Rilke, who wrote about creating his own star stories:

The most visible joy can only reveal itself to us when we've transformed it, within. There, look, the Rider, the Staff, and that fuller constellation they call Fruitgarland. Then further towards the Pole: Cradle, Way, the Burning Book, Doll, Window.

Like Rilke, as the children and I spun our tales we transformed our feelings about the stars, changing them from remote objects to something nearer, something that was ours.

There was genuine sadness among the children on the day I announced the observatory would be closing, and that we would be ending our study of space. A month had passed, and it seemed wise to end before the children's interest in astronomy set.

## Astronomers Already

Reflecting on and evaluating curriculum is an important exercise for teachers to undertake. This is how we learn; how we can make the next unit better. In this spirit I asked myself: was the astronomy curriculum a success? To answer my question I had to clarify the criteria for making a judgment.

One criterion that I am attracted to is that success should be gauged by how much the children have learned. Making this criterion operational generally comes down to ascertaining how much information the children gained;

for measurement purposes, how much information about a topic children can spew back to an adult. The weaknesses of such an evaluative approach are clear: the fallacy of equating facts gained with learning and the danger of valuing specific learning more than the disposition to learn. Nevertheless, I am a sucker for young children spouting facts, and am secretly proud when I hear my students reporting accurate information about a unit of study to parents or visitors. Despite my deeper understanding of what pedagogy involves, I want to say "See, they are learning something here in my classroom."

With the astronomy unit I had ample opportunity to feel proud. The children accumulated a vast store of information. Like junior Jeopardy contestants, they eagerly soaked up facts about the universe. The magnitude of information they absorbed became clear during our visit to the planetarium. After showing images of Jupiter and a comet, the astronomer innocently asked the children what they wanted to see. The flood gates were opened. The children cried out to see Mars, Pluto, Venus, nebulae, Ida the asteroid, Pegasus 51, and Betelgeuse. The astronomer was clearly impressed. Ending the presentation with his standard rap about how any of the children could grow up to be an astronomer, he stopped and added, "and it seems that some of you are astronomers already."

But just as becoming an astronomer involves more than accumulating facts, the success of a curricular unit involves more than children stockpiling information. More important to the success of curriculum is a second criterion: that units foster an interest in the material at hand, contributing to a positive attitude toward learning. Here I ask myself:

- Has the children's curiosity been piqued by the curriculum?
- Do they care about what is being presented?
- Are they hooked?

Of course, if children become interested in a topic they will gain information about it. But gaining information is the byproduct of reaching the prize, not the prize itself. Perhaps my valuation of process over product, children's disposition toward learning over information gained, should be reconsidered at some point in a person's education. But I stand firmly by my hierarchy regarding young children. Four- and five-year-olds will probably forget most of the information they learn in preschool. What I hope they retain is an inquisitive disposition, a love of learning.

It is here that our astronomy unit was clearly a success. Evidence of the children's passionate interest in space was everywhere. James' mother told me that she had to go to the library to get books on the universe in order to answer her son's constant questions about astronomy. On separate occasions,

Jack, Maddy, and Joy each approached me, excitedly telling me about how they had seen Orion the previous night. Max, whose socio-dramatic play had been mired in the middle ages for months, told his mother, "Mommy, Jack doesn't seem to like knights so much any more. He's more into the solar system. Me too." Even little Katie finally came around, making me drawings of the planets. The planetarium's astronomer was more correct than he knew; in their minds the children had become astronomers.

## Michael, the Moon, and Me

One night near the end of the astronomy unit, I left the day care center the same time as Michael. Out in the parking lot I caught a glimpse of the full moon rising, and called Michael over to see the sight. As anyone who has witnessed a moon rising knows, it was a beautiful scene. The moon appears larger than it does when it is higher in the sky, a huge sphere with an orangish tint. We watched together in silence for a few minutes, in awe of the moon's magnificence. And during those few minutes the gulf that existed between Michael and me disappeared. That gulf—the existential distance which separates us because of differences in age, experience, and the nature of our relationship— was in part the inevitable result of our teacher/student roles. When Michael was with me he was away from his parents, and I personified that separation for him. Like many children, the anger Michael felt about this separation was often projected onto me. But the gulf between Michael and me was wider, or more complicated, than what I experience with the typical child. There was closeness to be sure, but that closeness was often obscured by hostility. Michael was a child filled with anger. He talked about dynamiting the day care center and filling the preschool room with tarantula spiders to "get the teachers." I speculated about the source of Michael's hostility, but regardless of the source, a wide gulf existed between Michael and me.

At times, I am frustrated by such gulfs. At other times, I accept them as a fact of teaching. But during that moonrise, the gulf between Michael and myself temporarily melted away. We were just two people linked by our common appreciation of the full moon, experiencing the joy of discovering (and rediscovering) how beautiful it can be.

## Resources

Astronomy is one topic about which teachers should have little trouble finding useful material, with resources seemingly as abundant as the stars in the sky. For example, there are many non-fiction books for children on astronomy. Included in this list are Gail Gibbons' *The Planets* (New York: Holiday

House, 1993), Seymour Simon's *Our Solar System* (New York: Morrow, 1992), and Necla Apfel's *Nebulae: The Birth and Death of Stars* (New York: Lothrop, Lee & Shepard, 1988). These titles are chock full of information and beautiful photographs, but since many of the best books on astronomy have similar illustrations, they seem equally good. My recommendation is to go down to the public library and check out an armful. One book that does stand out, because of its wonderful story and because my group was so interested in asteroids, was *Meteor!* by Patricia Polacco (New York: Putman and Grosset, 1987).

Much of my information on the lore and science of the sky comes from the *National Audubon Society Field Guide to the Night Sky* by Mark Chartrand and Wil Tirion (New York: Knopf, 1995). The Guide describes, with supporting illustrations and photographs, the members of our solar system, nebulae, galaxies, and the stars. The section on the stars gives stories and factual accounts of the eighty-eight constellations. A more extensive guide, recommended for those truly devoted to the study of the sky, is Robert Burnham's *Burnham's Celestial Handbook: An Observer's Guide to the Universe Beyond the Solar System* (New York: Dover, 1978). More technical than the Audubon guide, this three-volume set holds enough information for years of study.

For in-depth information about our solar system, Tufts University astronomer Ken Lang has written two very readable texts: *Wanderers in Space: Exploration and Discovery in the Solar System* (Cambridge: Cambridge University Press, 1991); and *Sun, Earth and Sky* (Berlin: Springer, 1995). For those with a philosophical bent, Chet Raymo's *The Soul of the Night: An Astronomical Pilgrimage* (Saint Paul, MN: Hungry Mind Press, 1992) speaks to the wonder of the heavens and the spirituality of astronomy.

There is also a great deal of material available to teachers, both free of charge and for purchase. Resources and materials on space exploration and astronomy can be obtained without charge by writing to:

NASA Teacher Resource Laboratory
Mail Code 130.3
NASA Goddard Space Flight Center
Greenbelt, MD 20771
Phone: 301/286-8570

Further NASA materials are available in each state at the Regional Teacher Resource Centers. The location of these centers can be found in the catalogue available by writing to:

NASA CORE
Lorain County Joint Vocational School

15181 Route 58 South
Oberlin, OH 44074

The CORE catalogue is full of NASA produced audiovisual materials available for purchase. Two other reputable suppliers of space resources—maps, slides, books, posters, and videos—are available from:

Sky Publishing Corp.
49 Bay State Rd.
Cambridge, MA 02138
617/864-7360

Astronomical Society of the Pacific
390 Ashton Ave.
San Francisco, CA 94122
415/337-1100

For those online, there are a host of websites offering an array of resources, from curriculum ideas to the latest images from the Hubble Space Telescope. A sampling of possibilities include:

NASA SpaceLink
http://spacelink.msfc.nasa.gov

Public Access to NASA's Planetary Data
http://stardust.jpl.nasa.gov/public

Astronomy On-line: Ask Dr. Sue
http://dlt.gsfc.nasa.gov/ask

Astronomical Society of the Pacific
http://www.physics.sfsu.edu/asp/asp.html

Space has inspired a great deal of music, from Mozart's "Twinkle, Twinkle Little Star" to Elton John's "Rocket Man." Of the compositions mentioned in this essay, Van Morrison's "Moondance" is available on the album of the same name (Warner, 1970) as well as the greatest hits album *The Best of Van Morrison* (Exile, 1990). Bobby McFerrin sings a version of the tune on *The Van Morrison Songbook* (Connoisseur, 1997). Greg Brown's "Rooty, Toot, Toot for the Moon" is on his *One More Goodnight Kiss* disc (Red House Records). Gustav Holst's orchestral work *The Planets* has been recorded numerous times. Leonard Bernstein's New York Philharmonic performance (CBS, 1985) offers a fine rendition. My class' favorite planet was Jupiter. Subtitled "The Bringer of Jollity," it is an eminently danceable, heartwarming piece.

Finally, for those interested in introducing their class to astronaut cuisine, selected dishes eaten on NASA flights (ice cream sandwiches and Neapolitan ice cream slices) can be purchased from:

NASA Lewis Research Center
Exchange Store
21000 Brookpark Rd.
Cleveland, OH 44133
216/433-2985
http://gemini.lerc.nasa.gov/cfo/exchange/afood/asp

The shuttle astronauts also snack on a mixture of dried fruit and nuts. I am told the trail mixes available at local grocery stores are similar to what is eaten in space.

## Acknowledgements

I want to thank Ron Dandowitz of Boston's Charles Hayden Planetarium and Ken Lang of Tufts University for their contributions to my class' study of astronomy.

# 3
—

## *Hoop Dreams: Basketball*

### Hoop Dream Circa 1967

In my mind I hear the announcer's voice drone over the radio:

> Welcome back to McGaw Hall, home of the Northwestern Wildcats. Well one thing's for certain, no one expected our Wildcats to be this close so late in the game. They trail the unbeaten UCLA Bruins by a point with ten seconds left on the clock. NU gets the ball back after the time out, giving The Cats one last chance to complete an amazing comeback. The horn sounds and the teams are back on the court. The ball's inbounded to NU's point guard Ben Mardell. Mardell dribbles up court. He's picked up by All-American Lucius Allen. Mardell twirls and gets around Allen. What a move! Mardell darts into the lane. Seven-foot-tall Lew Alcindor jumps out to defend him. Mardell dribbles to the corner. Just three seconds left. Alcindor's playing tight defense. Mardell fakes a pass. One second left. Mardell shoots over Alcindor's outstretched arm, and . . . It's good! It's good! The Wildcats win!!! The Northwestern Wildcats have upset the defending national champions on a last second shot from the corner by Ben Mardell.

It takes me five tries, but I finally sink the shot from the corner of the driveway. It is 1967. I am seven years old. This was my hoop dream.

### Why Basketball?

There is a buzz of activity in my classroom. Juliet, Michael, Miriam, Dan, and Samantha are working on a life-size painting of Manute Bol. At seven-feet-seven-inches Manute is the tallest person ever to play in the National Basketball Association, and his figure stretches the length of the art area. Jack, Kevin, and Janet are in the book area playing "Bulls versus Lakers," a board game developed by our student teacher Jackie Rosenbloom. The children roll a die, then tally how many points their team has scored. Jack whoops in delight as his team pulls ahead. Matt, Maddy, Joy, Zachery, and Max are in the block area—recently converted to a basketball court—practicing hoops. Matt cries out, "I'm Rebecca, I'm Rebecca," referring to Rebecca Lobo, the star center of the U.S. Women's Olympic Basketball Team. Adding to the excitement are Max's shouts of, "Go team!" each time a shot makes it through the four-foot-high basket.

This buzz is, for me as a teacher, a dream come true. These are the sights and sounds of children who love what they are studying. For two consecutive years we have studied basketball in my preschool class. Both years the unit connected with my students on a profound level, generating an enthusiasm for the topic which lingered long after our formal study was concluded. It is the children's excitement about basketball that inspired this essay; an essay that describes and evaluates two successive groups' investigations of the game. In the process, the essay considers:

- using stories to bring topics of study to life;
- tapping children's fantasy and play to further inquiry;
- teaching skills as a natural part of study; and
- extending the learning environment beyond the classroom.

Examining two years of curriculum also sheds light on teaching as a dynamic process involving experimentation, reflection, and continual revision.

I begin with the obvious question about this unusual topic of study: why basketball? The answer is simple, I love basketball. I love playing it, watching it, and talking about it. As a child I shot countless balls at a hoop mounted on our family's garage. As an adult I enjoy the physical challenge and comraderie of playing with and against my friends, all of whom have fading hoop dreams of their own. Important basketball games, the NCAA tournament and the NBA playoffs, are among the few occasions during the year I watch TV. But I also enjoy taking in the city league games near my house, appreciating a neighbor's good pass or defensive hustle. And just ask my opinion about who was a better player, Larry Bird or Michael Jordan. There's a good discussion in the making. Or let me tell you about the time I saw Dr. J play.

For those who have read the chapter on astronomy or South Africa or the Talking Heads, it will come as no surprise that my love of the game was the initial inspiration for our basketball units. By bringing one of my passions into the classroom I could transmit enthusiasm for the topic of study and model a genuine joy of learning. Basketball was a subject where the children and I could be fellow learners, sharing questions, answers, information, and excitement. I felt that studying basketball would strengthen the children's sense that they, or more accurately we, were part of a community of learners, a group of people actively exploring the world around us.

Of course, my interest in basketball was not sufficient rationale for making the sport the focus of a unit of study. The children's interests, or potential interests, also had to be considered. Part of the task in choosing topics for exploration is identifying themes that connect with young children's underlying emotional concerns. Building curriculum around these concerns captures children's attention and maintains their interest in the units of study. I felt basketball would be a compelling topic for my charges because the subject connects with three primary preschooler concerns: power, competition, and the adult world.

Power—exercising power, desiring power, feeling powerful, and feeling powerless—is a central emotional issue of the preschool years. The dualistic nature of preschoolers' experiences with power is a source of great tension as children struggle with their feelings, hopes, and fantasies. On the one hand, children are becoming more skillful and competent, in many ways more powerful. They take great pleasure from their growing mastery. Being able to write one's name, or tie one's shoes, or shoot a basket is cause for continual celebration. On the other hand, children are increasingly aware of their limitations, of their powerlessness. Not being able to read, or tie one's shoes, or cross the street alone is cause for continual frustration. It is no wonder that power is a central theme of preschoolers' fantasies, with powerful figures— dinosaurs, superheroes, and parents—the dominant characters in their play. Three-, four-, and five-year-olds are fascinated by the big, strong, and powerful. For this reason, basketball players are of intrinsic interest to preschoolers.

The central drama of basketball, the game, relates to a second primary concern of preschoolers: competition. Being the fastest, the biggest, the most famous, and, of course, the first are dominant preschooler desires. This is why Shirley Hughes' picture book *Alfie Gets in First* (New York: Lothrop, Lee, and Shepard, 1982), a story about a three-year-old's compulsion to get into his house before his mother and little sister, rings so true. From what I have seen of their reactions to losing, I imagine many preschoolers would even be sympathetic to the famous statement, wrongly attributed to football coach Vince Lombardi, that "Winning isn't the most important thing, it's the only thing." This doesn't mean that as responsible caregivers we don't begin the long process of helping children learn to understand, channel, and moderate their competitive yearnings. But preschoolers' competitive zeal is real. We can try to stifle it, promote it, or ignore it, but competitiveness is part of what being four is all about. As teachers, we can use this concern to our advantage, as a hook into curriculum. Basketball involves winning, and this facet of the game attracts preschoolers.

Preschoolers are also beginning to look beyond their immediate surroundings, becoming interested in the larger adult world. Being conversant in topics adults value, and being able to contribute information to adult discussions, is highly satisfying to three-, four-, and five-year-olds. Basketball is important to many grown-ups, and is the subject of many adult conversations (particularly in March during the NCAA tournament and again in June during the NBA finals). As children move from toddlerhood into the preschool years, talking about hoops can replace peek-a-boo games as a way of connecting with adults.

Ultimately, a curriculum topic must be worthy of study. Part of my sense of basketball's worthiness involves the values that can be conveyed while discussing the game. Basketball is difficult to master, invoking the importance of hard work and practice in order to develop skills. Basketball has a set of rules to ensure the smooth running of the game and players' safety and invoke a sense of fairness and fair play. Basketball is a team sport, calling forth cooperation: only through working together can a team win. This is true for superstars as well as for average players. Jesse Jackson has noted that part of the greatness of Michael Jordan is that he understands, "The biblical injunction: the strong should bear the infirmities of the weak. [In this way] the strong do not get weaker—the weak get strong, and the strong get stronger" (*New York Times Magazine,* April 21, 1996, 44).

Last, but not least: *basketball is fun.* We were in the middle of a long, cold New England winter. We needed to study something that was fun.

## The Man in the Black-and-White-Striped Shirt

Despite the compelling rationale for studying basketball, I was hesitant to actually proceed with this unusual topic. My self-censor, what my friend Danny calls, "The Man in the Black-and-White-Striped Shirt," was cautioning me about undertaking something so off the beaten path in early childhood education. Would the parents approve? What would my student teacher and her supervisor think? Wouldn't it be better (read, safer) to study dinosaurs again? Sophisticated psychological creature that I am, I disguised my internalized referee in rationalist clothing, developing seemingly reasonable "concerns" about the topic. These concerns, which were threefold, almost cancelled our basketball season before it began.

To begin, I was wary of bringing a topic so laden with commercialism and hype into my classroom. Despite my love of the game, I recognize that the attention and acclaim given star players is completely out of proportion to what is reasonable or just. Sports in general, and basketball in particular, hold a far-too-sacred place in the pantheon of our culture, I self-consciously preached to myself. Not until I reminded myself that our focus would be on the game and not the hype, that we were studying basketball and not the kind of shoes Shaquille O'Neal wears, did I let go of this concern.

Gender lay at the heart of my second concern. Power, competition, and interest in the adult world—the emotional issues intended to hook children into basketball—are sterotypically male concerns. While girls are interested in power, their interest generally manifests differently than does boys'. For example, powerful creatures such as dinosaurs and superheroes are often not as compelling to girls as they are to boys. Winning and being first are usually not as vital to girls as they are to their male counterparts. And while many women play and enjoy watching basketball, the sport is still often perceived as a man's game; something many girls are not encouraged to discuss with their elders. I worried that basketball would engage my boys but leave the girls on the sidelines. A legitimate concern, but one I eventually realized called for outreach for the girls rather than abandonment of the topic.

My final concern revolved around the complex issue of race. Since the vast majority of professional basketball players are African American, studying basketball was almost sure to bring up the question "Why do most basketball players have dark skin?" I was uneasy about fielding this question because I didn't have a good answer. Talking about the intricate social and economic forces that dictate in the current racial mix of the NBA was well beyond the grasp of my students. I worried that highlighting basketball would perpetuate cultural stereotypes about African Americans. In particular, I was afraid the children might adopt the simplistic view that dark-skinned people are more athletic, but less cerebral, than their lighter-skinned counterparts. Moreover, knowing hoop dreams are not always benign, I wanted the African American boys in my class to understand that their life options went beyond sports.

Eventually, I realized I was guilty of projecting adult concerns onto the children. There was no reason my students would make any association, positive or negative, between athleticism and intelligence. Further, there was no reason to protect my students from a job category where African Americans often set the standard of excellence (though it was important for the children to see adults from a range of backgrounds as role models for each topic we studied).

This is not to say considerations about race are inappropriate when evaluating potential curriculum. The realities of our society demand that teachers ask such questions. In this case, however, my concerns were misplaced. When the question of the NBA's racial mix did come up, I responded that this was a complicated question, and apologized that I didn't have a good way to explain this to preschoolers. This seemed to satisfy my charges, who were far more interested in other facets of the game.

In the end, there was no reason not to study basketball. The man in the black-and-white-striped shirt had been placated. It was time for the first "season" to begin.

## The First Season: Rebecca Lobo and the Sarahs

It was the first day of our basketball unit. With the children gathered in the book area I held up a photograph of Rebecca Lobo. The picture of the six-foot-four-inch-tall Lobo is a striking image. Miriam, Matt, and Zack immediately clamored to know, "Who's that?" My ploy had worked. Having captured the children's attention, I began my tale:

> This is Rebecca Lobo, one of the best basketball players in the world. Rebecca started playing basketball when she was just a little bit older than you are. Her family had a basketball hoop, and she would play with her brother and her dad. Rebecca loved playing basketball, and she practiced and practiced.

Fast-forwarding through the next fifteen years, I mentioned Rebecca's play in junior high and high school and summarized her All-American career at the University of Connecticut, which culminated in her selection to the U.S. Olympic Basketball "Dream Team." But the real excitement began when I recounted a game Rebecca had played while still in college. Embellishing a bit, I explained:

> The Huskies hadn't lost a game all year, but that night they were in very big trouble. Syracuse was playing really well. With only a minute left in the game the Huskies were losing by five points. Their coach called a time out. He had a meeting with his team, and they made a plan. The plan was to get the ball to Rebecca. Back on the court the plan worked perfectly. A teammate passed Rebecca the ball. She soared into the air and shot. It was good. Now UConn was down by 3 points. They needed the ball back, but Syracuse had the ball. Out of nowhere Rebecca stole the ball away, and scored another basket! Now the Huskies were only down by 1 point, but there were

just a few seconds left in the game. A Syracuse player had the ball, and was dribbling down court. All Syracuse had to do was to hold on to the ball, and they would win the game. Now this is amazing. Rebecca stole the ball again! She dribbled, shot the ball, and . . . It was good! The Huskies had won.

A cheer rose up from the children. With that basket Rebecca Lobo became a class icon, a persona the children would put on when they began playing basketball.

I often begin planning units of study by identifying stories to tell the children about the subject. Stories help bring a topic of study to life. They are an important way for children to gain information about the world. Stories also provide fuel for many preschoolers' favorite activity: dramatic play. In telling stories about basketball, I was supplying the children with the raw material from which to form their own hoop dreams.

I chose Rebecca Lobo as the protagonist for the first basketball story because she was the type of person the children would find compelling: a star player on a winning team. She was also the type of person I felt comfortable forwarding as a hero: an intelligent, studious person (she was a scholastic All-American) who took her fame in stride. From all that I read it was clear Rebecca is a class act. Finally, the story of Rebecca established beyond dispute that girls play hoops.

As the unit unfolded over the next three weeks I told a score of basketball stories. Some were yarns spun to pass the time on long walks or while waiting for a late parent to arrive. Others were planned narratives connected to the curriculum and told at story time. Included in this category was the fascinating tale of Manute Bol. The story recounted Manute's childhood in the Sudan (where, according to legend, he had killed a lion), his recruitment by an American basketball scout because of his incredible height, and his motivation for coming to the United States (being able to send a substantial part of his salary home to promote rural development). The class' favorite story was a fantasy involving Rebecca Lobo, her Dream Teammates, and the children themselves. The tale began with the Dream Team losing a vital game. In deep trouble, Rebecca called upon the preschoolers for help. Without hesitating, the children came to the rescue. Excitement built as I described how each preschooler scored a critical basket. The children applauded each other and themselves as they led Rebecca's team to victory.

Their imaginations fired by stories, the children's natural inclination was to play. Anticipating this, my curriculum planning involved imagining what props might enrich the quality of the children's dramatic play. For basketball, the essential props were balls and a basket. Because our play yard was blanketed by snow, I constructed an indoor court in the block area using masking tape to demarcate the foul line. I purchased a commercial children's basket and adjusted it to its lowest setting (four feet) to allow for easy scoring.

The children flocked to the court. As they played it was quickly apparent that most of them had little prior experience with basketball. Dribbling and passing were foreign concepts, and they had no idea that there are two teams which alternate playing offense and defense. The children moved around the court with much urgency but little planning. They were ready to become Rebecca Lobo, but they hadn't a clue what Rebecca Lobo did.

The children's lack of basketball acumen wasn't a problem in itself. Preschoolers certainly don't need to be well versed in the rules and regulations of basketball. I did worry, though, that the chaos occurring in the block area would soon lose its appeal. The initial excitement over using the basketball court was sure to wear off if I didn't provide the children with some sense of what basketball involved to sustain and enrich their play.

Enter "basketball practice." On the third day of our hoops unit I explained to the class that included in the exploration time choices would be basketball practice. Because of limited space, I capped the number of participants at five. Oversubscribed on that and several successive days, the practices were organized into fifteen-minute sessions in order to allow all takers an opportunity to participate. The first session brought Matt, Joy, Maddy, and Dan to the basketball court. I greeted them with my basketball coach persona. Speaking in a deep, gravelly voice, I instructed:

> OK, team. Everyone line up on the foul line. That's right, the line's right here. Looking sharp. Good hustle, good hustle. Get in line.

With Joy and Dan looking very serious, and Matt and Maddy giggling some, I walked the children through some low-key drills on dribbling and passing. After about five minutes, I stopped structuring the practice, letting the children play as they wished. Joy, who was not known for her athleticism, turned out to be the class' best dribbler. She took great pleasure in working on that skill. Matt, Maddy, and Dan began shooting at the basket. I continued to bark out comments peppered with basketball terms—"three-pointers," "swish," "dunk." Of course, my coaching style bore little resemblance to a bellicose taskmaster such as Bobby Knight. There was no failure here: one bounce was a successful dribble. But the drama of coach and players seemed important to the children.

Indeed, drama and fantasy was often how children entered the world of basketball. Throughout the first season's activities the children never actually played basketball. What they did, and did with great gusto, was *play* at playing basketball. The distinction is an important one because to expect preschoolers to play hoops is unfair. The physical skills involved are too difficult and the rules of the game are too involved. The best illustration of this distinction came one day when we visited a local playground which had a basketball court. The children ran onto the court at once and began to play at playing basketball. A grand time was had by all as the children ran up and down the court, swishing imaginary three-pointers and converting pretend slam dunks. Often the two events happened simultaneously during ongoing multiple pretend games. The introduction of a real ball, meant to enhance the play, had the completely opposite effect. The ball caused reality to intrude on the play. Now shots really could be made or missed. And now only one player at a time could shoot. Everyone wanted the ball. Sharing proved difficult, and no one could make a basket on the ten-foot hoop. The children soon became frustrated, lost interest in the game, and abandoned basketball in favor of the playground's swings and climbing structure.

As the children became more involved in their basketball fantasies, they yearned for a greater degree of authenticity, if not reality, in their play. Perhaps because we had looked at many pictures of basketball players in action, uniforms became emblematic of this authenticity. To fulfill their desire, I helped the children create their own uniforms. Each child received a T-shirt. Using permanent markers, they decorated their shirts with a number, their name, and various designs. Cal drew stripes on his shirt, reminiscent of the Orlando Magic's jerseys. Janet drew flowers on her shirt. My contribution was to write our team name across the front of the jersey. Just as firefighter play is promoted by providing fire helmets, basketball play was promoted by providing uniforms. The children put on their jerseys, got on the basketball court and, in their minds, became basketball players.

Of course, in order for me to write our team name on the uniforms we needed to have a name. Recalling the selection process never fails to bring a smile to my face. Our discussions of basketball had touched on a number of team names, and when I broached the subject the children were enthusiastic about the prospect of selecting a name of their own. At a meeting we brainstormed suggestions. Included in our list were familiar designations: the Bulls, the Hornets, and the Magic. Also included was one wildly unusual name: the Sarahs. Why "the Sarahs" was suggested remains a mystery to me. While Sarah is Maddy's mother's name, the suggestion came from Janet. In any event, after a series of votes the Sarahs emerged as the group's top choice.

The children were completely unselfconscious about their unique selection. They wore their uniforms with pride, and were delighted to be part of the Sarahs. While this was a tightly knit group, being on the same team further heightened the children's esprit de corps.

My curriculum planning for basketball included activities involving subject areas (math, literacy, music, and art) important for preschoolers to experience. In my classroom there is no formal mathematics, art, or reading instruction. I never sit the entire group down to learn to count to ten, or give out worksheets on forming the letter *T*. This is not because preschool children should not be exposed to those subjects—they should. Rather, their exposure should come within a context as a natural part of some investigation or unit of study. By integrating math or literacy into units of study the utility of these skills becomes clear to children. Counting or reading or drawing connected to "real" activities become meaningful ways for children to learn. Decorating worksheets with basketball motifs doesn't count. Fortunately, in the study of basketball, math, art, music, and literacy naturally came into play.

Math was the easiest subject to link to the study of basketball. Scoring quickly brought addition into play. Depending on children's skill level, they either simply kept track of the number of baskets made or began counting, with the assistance of an adult, by twos and threes. Number recognition also naturally occurred. As a prominent feature of uniforms, numbers were used to identify favorite players. More advanced mathematics appeared in the collection and organization of data. Cathy and I introduced statistics—beloved by students of sports—in two ongoing graphs kept in the classroom. For several weeks Cathy tracked Shaquille O'Neal's scoring. The number of points Shaq scored in each of seven games was marked on a bar graph, allowing for a visual comparison of the magnitude of the different numbers. In the afternoon we graphed preferences about Dennis Rodman's hair color (at that time simply white, green, or red). Rodman, a flamboyant rebounder for the Chicago Bulls, frequently changed the color of his hair. The children were amused by his clownlike fashion statements, and asked visitors to our room to register a preference. Red emerged as the favorite, a fact we transmitted to Mr. Rodman via letter.

The collection of basketball statistics helped us branch into literacy and language arts. Data about Shaquille's scoring came from the box scores in the daily newspaper. The newspaper, we discovered, also had articles about basketball games and favorite players. Recognizing a place for rhythm and rhyme, our student teacher Jackie taught the class two basketball cheers. The first was a simple chant which began:

> Potato chip, potato chip, munch, munch, munch.
> We think the Sarahs are a mighty fine bunch.

A second, longer cheer was sung in a call and response form:

> Hey all you Sarah fans,
> Stand up and clap your hands.
> Now that you're in the beat,

> Stand up and clap your feet.
> Now that you're in the groove,
> This time let's really move.
> Ah oooh ga! Ah oooh ga!
> One, two, three, four, five,
> The Sarah team don't take no jive.

The children sang these cheers with much zest.

We also connected art projects to basketball. This included the previously mentioned life-sized picture of Manute Bol. As a statement that one did not have to be a giant to be an accomplished basketball player, the class made a similar portrait of Mugsy Bogues (at the time, the five-foot-four-inch guard was the shortest player in the NBA). Collages using photographs culled from the local newspapers also proved popular. The collage photos prompted many interesting basketball conversations.

But the uncontested highlight of our unit was a visit to the practice of a bonifide basketball team. The visit was easily arranged; I simply called the basketball coach at the nearest college team, who graciously invited us to watch her team. We arrived at the gym midway through the practice, and sat at half court as the team scrimmaged. At first the children sat silently, mesmerized by the play. When some of the awe wore off, the children expressed an interest in joining the action. Trying to accommodate this desire, I let the children run wind sprints on the sideline as the team ran through this drill on the court. I never saw Miriam and Samantha run so fast.

When the practice ended the players came over to say hello. It was as if the gods had come down from the heavens. The children were starstruck. The players were wonderful with the class, and they soon had the children chatting and even playing hoops. To end our visit we sang our basketball cheers, to the delight of the players. If it hadn't happened already, their encounter with these real players hooked the children on basketball.

The first season produced tremendous excitement about basketball. The sentiments of Helen were not uncommon. Prior to studying basketball, Helen aspired to be "a doctor for undersea animals and a dancer." After the hoops curriculum, Helen dreamed of being, "A doctor for undersea animals, a dancer, and Rebecca Lobo."

## The Second Season: Sarah Russell and the Crimson Bulls

One year later we were again studying basketball. To begin the second season the block area has once more been transformed into a basketball court. I have begun telling basketball stories. And we have a very tall visitor.

At six-feet-two-inches, Sarah Russell is a commanding presence in the classroom. The power forward has arrived neatly dressed in the red-and-black warm-ups of her team, the Harvard Crimson. I invite Sarah to join our meeting time, where it is quickly apparent that along with her athletic abilities Sarah has experience with youngsters. She talks naturally and warmly to the class, taking seriously the questions that most intrigued these young children, including, "Do basketball players eat during games?" and "What happens when the basketball hits you in the face?" At exploration time she draws a large crowd to the basketball court, giving pointers and encouragement to an adoring group of preschoolers eager to try basketball. Before leaving Sarah signs one of our balls, "No. 35 Sarah Russell," making the blue basketball our class' most precious possession.

Sarah's visit permanently silenced comments like "girls can't play basketball," and was an important part of my game plan for the second go-round of studying hoops. In embarking on a second season I was faced with an interesting challenge. Half the class (Maddy, Michael, Max, Jack, Janet, and Joy) were repeat preschoolers. Having participated in the first season, these children were keen on studying hoops, virtually demanding that the subject be a topic of study. They were also basketball savvy. The other half of the group— Joseph, Robert, Katie, Denaea, Kim, Nichole, and James—were going through their first preschool year and had little knowledge of, interest in, or even awareness of the game. James was outright hostile to the idea of studying basketball, hoping we would continue our investigation of astronomy. I knew that making basketball fresh for the veterans—myself included—and capturing the rookies' interest in the topic would be a challenge.

During the second season I repeated elements from the preceding year. To help draw my new students into the curriculum, we emphasized stories and dramatic play; basketball practices reappeared during exploration time to help supply the new students with a sense of basketball; math, literacy, art, and music became part of our investigation. To help keep my "old" students interested, I focused much of our study on specific teams, using suggestions from me and the children. Our focus on the Harvard Women's Basketball Team (the Crimson) was my contribution. Our focus on the Chicago Bulls came from my students. The impact of these additions was apparent as the children voted for their team name. The choice for the second season: the Crimson Bulls.

The focus on the Crimson was an outgrowth of our successful visit to the team practice the previous year. I felt with more preparation the visit this year could be even more meaningful. I was confident the team would interest my new students, while taking the investigation further would prove compelling for my old students. This led to a phone call to Kathy Delaney-Smith, the head coach of Harvard's team, a couple weeks before our study of basket-ball began. As in the preceding year, Kathy was very friendly and helpful. It was through her good offices that Sarah Russell paid a visit to our classroom. And it was through her that I again arranged a visit to a Crimson practice.

Our second visit with the Crimson was even more successful than the first. I had learned to gauge the children's attention span for such a visit, and we arrived nearer to the end of the practice. More important, the children now had a friend on the court—Sarah Russell. "There's Sarah!" they excitedly whispered when they saw Number 35 in action. When Sarah surreptitiously waved to us during a break in a scrimmage, the children swooned. Soon the entire group was shyly waving at Sarah as she set picks and pulled down re-bounds. After the practice Sarah and her teammates came over to say hello. "Maddy, this is Coach Smith," Sarah began as she introduced her new preschool friends to the team. The children's eyes shone with pride as Sarah called out their names.

But the best was yet to come. For our annual room social event I sug-gested going to a Crimson game. Never having been to a Crimson game, I knew this proposal was a bit of a risk and was naturally apprehensive about tampering with so many families' weekends. Still, I recalled from my youth the thrill of attending Northwestern games with my father and felt there was a good chance for a successful outing. So one Saturday evening almost the entire class and their parents crossed the Charles River to Briggs Arena in Boston. Even Joy's family, who hadn't attended a social event in four years, came after some cajoling. Returning to the scene of the practice, now filled with a throng of noisy fans, gave the children quite a charge. Just being in the stands and getting snacks at the concession stand was exciting. The action on the court was of interest as well. When Sarah Russell came into the game during the second half the children let out a loud hoot. We unfurled a "Go Crimson" banner and sang our cheers. Though the outcome was no longer in doubt, Harvard cruising to a 102–74 victory over Brown, the preschoolers screamed each time Sarah touched the ball. After the game the children and their families went out on the court to congratulate Sarah. James was particularly happy to see Sarah again, but thought it curious that "Every time I see Sarah Russell she is very sweaty." Sweaty, and very pleased to greet her loyal fans.

It was complete serendipity that we were following the Crimson in the midst of an historic season. The win over my alma mater brought Harvard to 13–0 in league play, putting them one victory away from a never-before-achieved undefeated Ivy League season. On the Monday following the game I brought a large graph of the conference standings to meeting time. I inter-preted the standings, how the team on the top is in first place, the next team down is in second place, and so on. Then, focusing on the win-loss columns, I explained:

> Now after the victory against Brown you can see how many games the Crimson have won (cries of "thirteen" from the children as I pointed to the number). And how many they have lost (cries of "zero"). Now there are fourteen games in the season, so the Crimson have one game left to play. To-morrow night the Crimson play Dartmouth, the Big Green. If they win that game they will have won all their games. No team in the history of the Ivy League has ever done that.

The next day, the day of the big game, I continued the story:

> Now a few years ago, near the end of the season, the Big Green was also 13–0. And they were hoping to be the first team to be undefeated in the Ivy League. They only had one game left, and you know who they had to play? The Crimson.

I went on to detail how Harvard had played the spoiler that year, and why Dartmouth now yearned for revenge. If Sarah Russell and company played as a team, I concluded, they had a good chance to win and go down in the record books.

The children were captivated by the unfolding drama. Grabbed by the excitement myself, I went to Tuesday night's game. In a hard-fought battle Harvard came away with the win. I reported in a grave voice the next day to a very attentive group of children:

> It was a very tough game last night. As you remember, the Big Green really wanted to stop the Crimson from getting that fourteenth victory. From the start they played really hard. Each time the Crimson would take the lead the Big Green would score a few baskets. Again and again. Back and forth. The Crimson. The Big Green. It was a very close game. But in the end, the Crimson began scoring a lot of baskets. Sarah Russell came into the game and scored some baskets. The final score was the Big Green 57 and the Crimson . . . 75. The Crimson won! They are undefeated!

Spontaneous applause broke out. Children high-fived each other in celebration. I continued, my serious tone replaced by an upbeat recounting:

> After the game the team got out a ladder, and put it under the basket. One by one the players climbed the ladder and cut a cord of the net. After each player had a turn, the coaches went up. Finally, the net was hanging by just one string. Coach Smith went up the ladder and cut the net down. Every-one cheered! But when she got down the ladder some of the players had a surprise for her. They dumped a big bucket of water on her head.

Needless to say, the children were very happy about the game's results. James was very impressed by the whole affair. He reported to his parents the significance of Harvard's achievement, noting, "Nobody's ever gotten fourteen wins in the Ivy League, not since the dinosaurs." For days afterward the children talked about the Crimson, their undefeated season, and the bucket of water on Coach Smith's head.

Concurrently, there was much talk about Michael Jordan and the Chicago Bulls. The talk originated mostly from Max, Jack, and Michael. The trio's interest in the Bulls had begun during our first season studying basketball. A native Chicagoan, I had talked some about my childhood team. Jack's father was also from Chicago, and his sports loyalties encouraged his son's interest. At the time, the Bulls were the most famous sports team on the planet, so there was a larger cultural context focusing attention on the team. The three boys' interest in the Bulls had percolated for a year, erupting into a full-blown passion when we began studying basketball a second time. Their passion was evidenced in their play. No more knights and dragons. No more swings or climbing structure. As soon as the opportunity arose, Jack, Max, and Michael were shooting hoops, pretending to be Michael Jordan and Scottie Pippen.

It was not only the quantity of basketball play that was impressive. The quality of Jack, Max, and Michael's play had changed from the previous year. Now five year olds, these three no longer played playing basketball. They were trying to *play* basketball. The change manifested itself in two ways. First, there was an intense drive to master the sport's basic skills. Jack spent countless hours practicing long shots: his "three pointers." At the end of the day Max would dribble up and down the play yard until his mother dragged him out the gate. Both boys' families reported an endless amount of basketball practice at home. Their persistence had its rewards. Jack's shot became extremely accurate, even from great distances, and Max could dribble competently with both hands. Second, there was a new awareness and concern about the rules of the game. The boys insisted the adjustable hoop be raised to its highest setting when they played to make the game more realistic. During their games it was no longer acceptable to carry the ball to the hoop, that was travelling. Shot blocking could not involve touching the rim, that was goal tending.

The insistence on fidelity to rules inevitably led to quarrels. The conflict over technical fouls is a case in point. Over a breakfast discussion with his father about Dennis Rodman and the Bulls, Jack learned about technical fouls. He arrived at day care all fired up about this rule called by referees to penalize unsportsmanlike conduct. That afternoon, playing one-on-one with Michael, he tested out the concept. Michael had the ball and was dribbling toward the hoop. "Technical foul!" Jack yelled. "What's that mean?" a perplexed Michael asked. "You have to give me the ball. And no arguing or you get more technical fouls," Jack answered confidently. Michael deferred to authority, and handed Jack the ball. On Michael's next possession Jack called another technical foul, and then another, and then another. Finally, reduced to tears, Michael sulked away from the game. While I give the children much latitude to work out their disputes, in this situation, with Michael deeply hurt and Jack confused about how to right the situation, I decided to intervene. I sat down next to Jack and asked him about technical fouls. He told me "Dennis Rodman gets a lot of them." I agreed, but pointed out only referees could call this infraction. Highlighting this aspect of the rule provided Jack a way out of the conflict. While initially wanting to use the new rule to assert his power, Jack was ultimately more interested in playing than arguing, and more interested in preserving a friendship than dominating the game. Jack invited Michael back to the court. He explained that only referees could call technical fouls, and promised, "There aren't any referees here."

Interest in rules, in playing the game the way it is "supposed to" be played, also led to a great deal of talk about winning and losing. When the boys played they really kept score, and I received excited reports from the games' victors. But playing basketball, as opposed to playing playing basketball, meant that along with the winners there would also be losers. Michael, whose basketball prowess wasn't at the same level as Jack or Max's, often came up short in the trio's contests. It was clear from his sorrowful face after these defeats that Michael wasn't taking the losses casually. Losing seemed even more painful for Max. While his losses were infrequent, when they did occur Max would burst into tears. My heart went out to Michael and Max. I felt badly that activities related to a unit of study were causing such hard feelings. While it was Michael and Max's decision to play basketball to win (and lose), it would be disingenuous to say I had no role in promoting this competition. In the stories I told about the Crimson and Rebecca Lobo, it was clear I valued winning. I was reinforcing general cultural attitudes toward competition, values I wasn't sure I wanted to perpetuate, and was unsure how to proceed. The complex issue of competition had come to the forefront of my class.

In deciding how to respond to competitive basketball I had to consider what I wanted for my charges regarding competition. Truth be told, my feelings were ambivalent. On the one hand, I wanted to maintain the positive sense of community that had been built in the classroom, and feared intense competition would undermine this. I also wanted to shield the children from the pain of losing. On the other hand, I didn't want the children to feel guilty about their competitive impulses, and shy away from activities where achievement might involve comparisons and implicit competition. Ultimately, I hoped my charges would grow up to enjoy competitive games, and fit into a society predicated on competition. Still, I hoped the new generation would be less competitive and more cooperative. And so on. Out of this internal dialogue I realized that there wasn't a right way to be regarding competition. Rather, what I wanted for my charges was for them to develop a healthy attitude toward competition; that they could enjoy winning, accept losing, and understand their feelings (and the feelings of others) about both.

What I wanted for the children regarding competition paralleled what I wanted for them regarding other charged issues which play out in the classrooms. While the nature of the concern was new, addressing difficult emotional issues was familiar territory. For example, at the same time Max and Michael were shedding tears over losing basketball games, there were numerous conflicts over friendship which we were addressing. Maddy and Janet were taking turns crying as they struggled over jealousy and exclusion in their relationship. Denaea was having tantrums at meeting times because she felt that no one was her friend. James and Michael were engaged in periodic skirmishes as James tried to integrate into the group and Michael strove to exclude him. And so on.

On the days when I hadn't gotten enough sleep, the tears, harsh words, and general dissidence created by these issues caused me to fantasize about banning both friendship and competition from my classroom. Of course I couldn't ban friendship, nor would I want to. On days when I was sufficiently rested, I relished the opportunity to help the children learn about and work through the difficulties in their relationships. The same was true of competition. Even if basketball hadn't existed, there still would have been competition. Michael, Jack, and Max competed over who got their jacket on first, who ran the fastest on the way to the park, and who finished cleanup first. While their intensity about winning created conflict, it also drew the three together. Banning competition would have taken away something that made their lives fun and exciting. Competition turned a walk to the park into an Olympic event, and even made cleanup times enjoyable.

While not part of my initial curriculum planning, the threesome's focus on winning basketball games provided an opportunity to help all the children learn about competition. Learning occurred in two venues. The first was on the court itself. Here my goal was to provide a safe, supportive environment to experience competition. In general, I gave the children much latitude to work out issues among themselves. Jack, Michael, and Max had a cumulative ten years' experience at the day care center. During these years they had received much coaching on expressing feelings and processing group dynamics. I let them use their skills to solve problems arising from competition. There were times I did intervene, when the boys were stuck (as with the technical foul scenario), or to work with a teachable moment. With Jack and Max, I focused on perspective taking, occasionally asking them to consider how Michael felt after their games, and how they might make him feel better. I let Michael know he didn't have to play basketball or could suggest that his friends play hoops in a noncompetitive way.

Meeting time discussions also provided an opportunity to learn about competition. Such discussions allowed the children to talk and think about competition, and let me gain a better understanding of what competition meant to the children. One such discussion was sparked by a contrived letter I wrote the group. At meeting time about a month after the conclusion of our formal study of basketball I announced that the group had mail. Always excited to receive letters, the children watched with much anticipation as I opened the envelope and read:

Dear Preschoolers,

I like winning, but is winning the most important thing? Would you still like me if I didn't win?

Sincerely,
Michael Jordan

After recovering from the shock of getting a letter from Michael Jordan, the children responded to the second question. Of course they would like Michael even if he didn't win. I tactfully avoided pointing out that the reason they liked Michael in the first place was that he did win a lot, and focused attention on the first issue: is winning the most important thing? Janet, Maddy, and Joseph were clear: winning wasn't the most important thing. Jack, Max, and Michael concurred, though there was uncertainty in their voices. To push the children's thinking a bit I asked some provocative questions:

*Ben:* Jack, which is more important, winning in basketball or getting a piece of chocolate cake?

*Jack:* Chocolate cake.

*Ben:* Max, which is more important, winning in basketball or having a sleepover at a friend's?

*Max:* A sleepover.

*Ben:* Michael, which is more important, winning in basketball or spending time with your mom on the family days?

*Michael:* Spending time with my mom.

Having established a consensus that winning wasn't the most important thing, I decided to push from the opposite direction. I stated, "So all these things are more important than winning. It sounds like winning isn't that important. So what happens when you lose? Without hesitation, though in a quiet voice, Michael answered, "I cry."

Michael's honesty was as refreshing as it was informative. Unlike some adults, these children knew winning wasn't the only thing. They also knew, and were not afraid to say, that it is really fun to win, and it is very painful to lose. Like the pain of being rejected by a friend, it is a pain that I sometimes wish we could banish from childhood. But that is not possible. The best we can do is help children begin to understand competition and their feelings about it, and hope they develop a healthy perspective on winning and losing.

Beyond their passion for playing, Jack, Max, and Michael also loved talking about and learning about the Bulls. When they came to day care with information about the previous night's game, I found myself in increasingly sophisticated conversations with them about basketball. To support their burgeoning knowledge I began bringing in the sports page to look over box scores with the three. Further support was provided by our student teacher, Jenn Carlson, a high school player who knew a lot about basketball. Jenn loved chatting about hoops with the children and was a willing participant in the ongoing basketball games occurring during free play. To help further our investigations, Jenn invited her father, a high school referee, to talk to the class. An amiable fellow, Richard Carlson arrived with his referee jersey and basketball rule book. Max, Michael, and Jack hung on every word of his presentation. After Richard's visit our basketball court was filled with shouts of "double dribble" and "palming."

Not everyone was so intense or as sophisticated about basketball, though everyone participated and enjoyed the unit. When Kim, Robert, and Michelle took the court their chaotic movements were of children who were playing playing basketball. I loved watching their play, knowing that in the not-so-distant future it would be replaced by something less fanciful and, in a way, less fun. Maddy and Janet enjoyed shooting hoops, but for minutes, not hours, at a time. During the three-week unit Katie never touched a basketball, though she did enjoy creating basketball collages. And the entire class, from my basketball aficionados to my mildly interested observers, knew who the Chicago Bulls were and were Harvard Crimson fans. Most important, they were all on the same team: the Crimson Bulls.

Their undefeated season and resulting Ivy League championship had earned the Harvard Crimson a berth in the NCAA tournament. Matched up against top seeded North Carolina, they were given little hope of advancing beyond the first round. Still, their fans in the preschool room were upbeat, sending them letters of encouragement. Despite our good wishes, the inevitable occurred. The loss to North Carolina ended the Crimson's storybook season. After I told the children the sad news Max raised his hand and asked me a very interesting question. "Do you still like the Crimson, or do you like North Carolina now?" It was a question that resonated among all the children, because I felt twelve pairs of eyes staring at me intently. I thought for a moment, and then responded:

> It seems that North Carolina is a better basketball team than the Crimson this year. But I still like the Crimson better. I like the Crimson because they are such nice people. Sarah Russell came to visit us. Then the team let us visit their practice, and we talked to Sarah after the game. So I'm still a Crimson fan.

I then posed the question to the children. Despite the loss, the children were also still Crimson fans.

## Tennis Anyone?

Both the first and second years of studying basketball were championship seasons, ranking among the most exciting units I have participated in. The level of engagement of the entire group was very high. The children would share information about the sport among themselves and with me, discussing, for example, how many points Michael Jordan had scored the night before. The group was enthusiastic about any project related to basketball. Hoops were on their minds, and throughout the day they asked insightful, probing questions about the game. For many months afterward, children referred to Rebecca Lobo, Manute Bol, Michael Jordan, and Sarah Russell.

The success of the basketball units created an interesting temptation to study another sport. The idea of studying additional sports was not mine, but came from some of my students and their parents. Max and Kevin asked when we could study baseball. Dan wanted to know about the possibilities of studying football. Michael's father thought that soccer would make a great topic of inquiry. I half expected someone to call out, "Tennis anyone?"

Max, Kevin, Dan, and Michael's dad were right. Baseball, football, soccer (and even tennis) would have made fine topics. With the study of basketball some of the children in my class decided there wasn't a sport they didn't like. With them, a unit on baseball or football would have been an instant success. Still, I resisted the temptation. Becoming involved in sports is a double-edged sword. There are wonderful possibilities in watching and playing, but there is a darker side as well. Sports can be an exciting diversion from mundane reality where heroic feats of determination, skill, and grace are displayed. Sports can unite people across racial and class lines. But sports can also become an obsession bordering on idolatry where priorities and values become badly skewed. Like the magic ring Bilbo Baggins discovered in J. R. R. Tolkien's *The Hobbit* (Boston: Houghton Mifflin, 1985), sports can provide a useful tool for the classroom teacher, but I fear, if tried on too often, can have a corrupting influence.

Larger ethical questions aside, in the end I was looking for a balance of dreams for my charges. Watching Matt as Rebecca Lobo or Max as Michael Jordan gave me great satisfaction. I was pleased that the children were developing hoop dreams, that the study of basketball enriched their fantasy lives. But I was wary of all their dreams involving sports heroes. I also wanted the children to learn about, and perhaps even dream about, being astronomers, musicians, wild-life biologists, and social activists.

## Hoops Dream Circa 1997

It's the Chicago Bulls fifty-eight, and the Utah Jazz twelve. Michael has the ball. He's guarded by Karl Malone. Michael passes it to Scottie. Scottie shoots a three pointer. It just misses, but the other Michael Jordan gets the ball. He runs by John Stockton. Slam dunk! Now the Bulls have fifty-eight, fifty-nine, SIXTY points! Utah has the ball, but Scottie steals it away . . .

This is the voice I imagine Max, Jack, and Michael hear inside their heads as they play hoops against Phil and Paul (Jack and Michael's fathers). It is a voice which pronounces Utah, "Ooh-tah." It is a voice which allows two Michael Jordans to be on the court.

For months the play yard has witnessed this intensive basketball game. I can tell time by it. If Phil and Paul are facing Michael Jordan (Max), Scottie Pippen (Jack), and Michael Jordan (Michael) it must be 5:30. On this particular day I watch Michael hand the basketball to Max, who in turn runs past Phil toward the basket. After he slams the ball through the hoop Max gets a high five from Michael and a hug from Jack. It seems that the game is over. The Crimson Bulls have won again. Max, Michael, and Jack's hoop dreams have come true.

## Resources

The most valuable experience in our two seasons of studying basketball, having the children meet real basketball players, should not be too difficult to arrange. High school and college teams are everywhere, so finding a team to visit is just a matter of making some phone calls. While my reception by Coach Smith and her players is no guarantee that every team will be so generous, my experience is that members of the community are often very open to sharing their talents with groups of children. The basketball season for high school and college generally runs from December through March. Some teams have media guides, which can be consulted to help familiarize the children with the team before a visit to a practice or game.

Print resources for the study of basketball can be collected with relatively little effort. With the advent of the WNBA (Women's National Basketball Association), professional basketball is being played nearly year-round. Often pictures of basketball players appear in connection with stories in the newspapers. The sports weekly *Sports Illustrated* is also a good source of basketball news and contains breathtaking action photos of players.

Local libraries are stocked with books about the game in both the adult and children's sections. In the children's section look for three recent picture books: Eloise Greenfield's *For the Love of the Game: Michael Jordan and Me* (illustrations by Jan Spivey Gilchrist [New York: HarperCollins, 1997]) uses Michael Jordan's hero status for the best purposes, encouraging children to try to achieve their fullest potential. *Swish* by Bill Martin Jr. and Michael Samon (illustrations by Michael Chesworth [New York: Henry Holt, 1997]) uses rhythm to tell a story of a women's basketball game. Robert Burleigh's *Hoops* (illustrations by Stephen Johnson [San Diego: Harcourt, Brace, 1997]) poetically describes the feel of playing basketball. All three books are the stuff of which hoop dreams are made. For more factual information *The Young Basketball Player* by Chris Mullins and Brian Coleman (London: Dorling Kindersley, 1995) has good explanations about the rules of the game. In general, peruse the sampling found catalogued under call number j796.323. While many titles here are geared for older children, the photographs in these books can prove useful.

In the adult section, volumes include information about the sport that can serve as the basis for stories, as well as photographs children can appreciate. There are biographies of basketball stars (e.g., *Manute: The Center of Two Worlds* by Leigh Montville [New York: Simon and Schuster, 1993]), as well as titles that recount the stories of specific teams (e.g., *The Boston Celtics: The History, Legends, and Images of America's Most Celebrated Team* by Bob Ryan [Reading, MA: Addison-Wesley, 1989]). Further thoughts on how adults can help children process winning and losing are found in Constance Kamii's (1980) *Games in Early Education: Implications of Piaget's Theory* (Washington, DC: National Association for the Education of Young Children).

At times I fear I perpetuate the image of the basketball player as incredibly tall. In fact, people of all shapes and sizes can enjoy the game. The next time we study basketball I plan to challenge the stereotypical image of a basketball player more directly by highlighting wheelchair basketball. A preliminary search suggests resources for such an endeavor can be found in two places. Photos of players appear regularly in the periodical *Sports and Spokes.* Actual players may be reached either through local chapters of the Paralyzed Veterans of America or the Cerebral Palsy Association.

I want to thank Coach Kathy Delaney-Smith and her players, especially No. 35 Sarah Russell, for enriching my class' study of basketball.

# 4

## The Case of Miss D.: Emotions

### Manny's Story

Early in my teaching career I worked as an assistant in a three-year-olds room at a day care center in Rhode Island. Manny was one of my students, an adorable little boy with big brown eyes and a mop of dark brown hair. He came from an Hispanic family, and I smiled each time he spoke to me in his heavily accented English. Manny's favorite color was red, and he loved his sandals, probably because he could put them on all by himself. But what I remember most vividly about Manny was that he was completely, totally miserable at school.

Manny had acute separation anxiety. Each morning he entered the classroom in tears. The crying persisted for up to thirty minutes after his parents said good-bye. When the crying finally stopped Manny would withdraw, sucking his thumb and refusing to participate in the daily activities. The only time I saw him smile was at lunch, when he could sit with his older brother in the center's cafeteria.

The head teacher's response to Manny's distress was straight out of the Watson/Skinner behavioral handbook. In order to avoid "reinforcing the behavior" (Manny's tears), she ordered the team not to respond to the crying. In no event were we to "baby him" by picking him up or otherwise comforting him. In an attempt to thwart Manny's habit of thumb sucking, she wrapped masking tape around his thumb.

I had just begun teaching, and did not have an articulated conception of children's emotional development. My intuition told me her approach was wrong, but I lacked the confidence needed to challenge my supervisor. While I did covertly untape his thumb, I followed the party line in my overall approach to Manny.

It was an approach doomed to failure. Manny continued to cry despite the absence of any reinforcement. He continued to be miserable, and his parents recognized this. After six weeks of crying they withdrew him from the center.

Over the years I have learned how to be more effective with children who are missing their parents. I find that responding to children's distress by reassuring them and holding them is generally the best strategy. Rather than reinforcing the crying, comforting helps build relationships that allow children to feel safe and secure in the classroom. Once they feel comfortable, we can proceed with the curriculum.

I felt that I had a pretty good handle on this aspect of teaching, even publishing two articles on the subject (Mardell, 1992, 1994). Then I met Denaea. Energetic, attractive, and completely forlorn, Denaea (nicknamed Miss D. by my co-teacher Cathy and I so we could confer with some degree of confidentiality in front of the children) manifested unhappiness that dwarfed any sadness presented by Manny. Teaching Miss D. was one of the greatest challenges I have faced in fifteen years in the classroom. My days with Miss D. often left me emotionally and physically exhausted. But in the end, working with Miss D. was a very gratifying experience that changed the way I teach.

This chapter is different from the other chapters in this volume in that it does not describe a particular curriculum unit or curricular activity. Rather, it describes my struggle to help one child and explains how this struggle expanded my approach to behavioral issues from beyond attempting to address misbehavior to confronting the underlying emotional distress. Despite this difference, the chapter has some important commonalities with the rest of the book. The story involves many of the children mentioned in previous chapters; hearing it gives a sense of what else was happening in the classroom as we studied basketball and squirrels. At its heart, this essay is about teaching and learning, but in this case the teaching and learning center around emotions— how people feel angry and sad, how they might best express these feelings, and how to help a group of children understand when someone in the class is communicating their feelings in inappropriate ways. Because helping children understand and grapple with emotions is an integral part of teaching preschoolers, I have included this story of Miss D.

# The Long Fall

A scream cut across the day care center. While I'd heard such wails from the Infant and Toddler Rooms, hearing it from the Stomper (three-year-old) Room next door was unprecedented. It was a desperate cry; a cry embodying anger, fear, and sadness.

This scream was how I met Miss D. Actually, I heard Miss D. before I heard about her. Not until the year's first staff meeting did I learn who was responsible for these acoustic disturbances. Throughout Miss D.'s year in the Stomper Room these screams persisted. They had a piercing quality which, sadly, became a regular feature of the center's ambient noise. As a teacher in the room Miss D. would be moving to next, I grew uneasy whenever I heard it. I was to find that my trepidations were well-founded.

Miss D. was visiting her father in Tennessee when the preschool year began in September. She arrived in our class two weeks later on her best behavior. Miss D. sat quietly during story times, moved easily from one activity to the next, and settled down quickly for nap. She did make an unusually large number of overtures for affection, initiating hugs with practically any adult that came into the room. But this was a problem I could live with. The transition into the preschool room was going so smoothly that by the third day I began thinking Miss D. had matured over the summer, outgrowing her regressed behaviors.

Of course, I should have realized that children don't simply outgrow the type of emotional crises that Miss D.'s Stomper-year outbursts signified. Day four reminded me of this fact. I learned later that the difficulties began early that day. At home, Miss D.'s refusal to get dressed brought a sharp rebuke from Toni, her mother. A tantrum ensued. After almost an hour Toni was finally able to cajole Miss D. out of the house. Late to work, Toni's good-bye at day care was brief, leaving her daughter in tears. When I arrived for my shift at 12:30 Miss D. was whining at Cathy, insisting that it was impossible for her to put the leftovers of her sandwich back into the lunch box. As I told a story to the group before nap, Miss D. was clearly out of sorts. She intentionally jostled the child next to her, laughed randomly, and paid no heed to the story.

Nap time was Armageddon. Just getting Miss D. to lie on her mat was exhausting work. Each step from the book area to the nap room (going to the bathroom, washing hands, taking off shoes, getting a blanket) was resisted. Her eventual arrival on the mat did not improve the situation. Soon after the lights went out the disruptions started. Miss D. began giggling, encouraging the children on the nearby mats, Joy and Janet, to do the same. I hushed all three, but within a minute Miss D. was giggling again. After several gentle reminders for quiet, I put on my strict teacher's voice and firmly told Miss D.,

"You have to stop. This is a quiet time. You need your rest to have a good afternoon, and it is not fair to the other children to disrupt their naps." My final point, about disrupting other children's naps, was clearly lost on Miss D. She exploded in histrionics. Here were the screams I had heard from the Stomper Room.

This was not the first time I had experienced tears in the face of a limit set. It is an interesting strategy for a child to employ, attempting to change from offending party to victim. I had learned that it is important to ignore these tears, keeping the focus on the original issue. After a few minutes, preschoolers generally recognize this approach is not bearing fruit, and will stop crying. My sense was that Miss D. was testing to see where tears would get her in the Preschool Room. I wanted to establish that when they came as part of an attempt to circumvent a limit, the answer was, not very far.

I had been prepared for this moment, and used the words Miss D.'s Stomper Room teachers used, with some success, under similar circumstances. I told her, "I would love to rub your back. I want to be with you, but you have to stop crying first." I then moved away and waited. And waited. And waited. It wasn't an easy wait, knowing that Miss D.'s screams were keeping thirty children throughout the center awake. I knew they were awake because it was impossible for anyone to sleep through these glass-shattering screams. A child that I was responsible for was depriving all these children of their critical midday rest. That fact weighed on me, and after fifteen minutes I gave in. Against my better judgment I took Miss D. outside to the play yard to bring quiet to the center, and to comfort her.

In a sense Miss D. had won, but she took no pleasure in her victory. She was inconsolable. I tried a variety of techniques to comfort her. I held her. I left her alone. I spoke calming words to her. All with little effect. Finally, forty-five minutes after the onset, the crying stopped.

Nerves frayed, I telephoned Cathy that evening. We agreed upon strategies concerning what words to use and what limits to set. We would try to give Miss D. much attention when she was acting appropriately, but would isolate and ignore her when she "tantrumed." We concluded that, despite the noise, it was critical to keep Miss D. in the nap room, so as not to reinforce her tantrums and so she could get some very necessary rest. To help implement this part of our strategy, I brought earplugs to work the next day.

I also spoke to Toni, who was not surprised by what I told her. Yes, she had seen this behavior before. Yes, she was concerned about it. I explained how impressed I was with Miss D.'s outburst, and how I could really use some help figuring out what to do. With Toni's consent, I called the local school department to arrange for a case worker to visit. My hope was to obtain some consultation for myself, and psychological services for Miss D.

The next few weeks were difficult. It was as if trump had been broken. We were seeing the real Miss D. Transitions between activities were resisted, often producing tantrums. Attendance at meetings was sporadic, either because Miss D. refused to attend or because she was so disruptive she was asked to leave. Nap times produced tears and screams, but the earplugs came in handy, and waiting the tantrums out eventually resulted in sleep. Miss D. was so exhausted by being Miss D. all morning that a nap was inevitable. Cathy and I maintained a consistent message, that we would take care of her, but Miss D. had to refrain from screaming. The situation was manageable, barely, and I desperately hoped that help was on its way.

After a month a school department official did visit the classroom. Her presence did little to restrain Miss D.'s more flamboyant behaviors, and she was treated to a high-decibel display. During the observation Miss D. was absent from meeting time and much of snack, standing in the block area screaming for her mother. She was able to calm down enough to eat some snack, but a second tantrum ensued when Miss D. found the destination for our walk not to her liking. Despite the outbursts, it was concluded that Miss D. did *not* qualify for assistance because her "behavioral issues did not impact her learning." Behavioral charts (sticker reinforcements for good behavior) and consistent limit setting by the classroom teachers was recommended. I was infuriated. It was clear that Miss D. was a special child who needed special help. She was missing most of the meeting times and many activities. Of course her behavior was affecting her learning; she wasn't there to learn. But there it was: no outside assistance. Cathy and I were officially on our own.

The leaves changed colors and began to fall. October made way for November. Patterns of behavior were established. Mondays were harder than other days for Miss D. Transition times were difficult. Wetting at nap became common. Tantrums were routine when returning to the center on walks. Antisocial behavior toward peers, abusive language, and spitting appeared. Midterm pressures for Toni in her graduate program resulted in more outbursts at day care for Miss D.

Somehow, though, working with Miss D. seemed a bit easier. This was partly because I now knew what to expect, and had become somewhat desensitized to her more outrageous behavior. There was also some incremental improvement in Miss D.'s functioning as she formed relationships with Cathy and myself. Months of consistency and caring were bearing some fruit. Still, there was a tremendous distance to travel. This was a little girl in crisis.

In order to travel that distance I felt there had to be some change in Miss D.'s life outside day care. In hopes of hastening this change, I arranged two parent conferences with Toni during the fall. The first was an emergency session in early October where Toni gave Cathy and I some details of her daughter's life. Toni explained she returned to work four weeks after giving birth to Miss D. The new baby was taken care of by one of Toni's eight sisters. Toni reported that Miss D. had always been "a difficult child"; difficult to sooth, a picky eater, irregular in napping patterns, and fitful in her sleep. It had been hard for Toni to bond with her daughter, who was very different from her son, an easygoing child now in third grade who excelled in school.

Toni interpreted Miss D.'s outbursts as a symptom of being "spoiled." She worried that, "All the time with her father this summer spoiled her even more. With him, she gets what she wants by crying, and is rewarded for real cutesy, immature behavior." I was not surprised to learn that at home Miss D. was often clingy and very needy, asking for a lot of attention. During the long history of this "manipulative behavior" Toni had been at times been "pushed to the breaking point," but was currently "ignoring the behavior."

I saw this conference as an initial step in building a relationship with Toni, and knew the conversation had to be continued. It was clear that Miss D. would benefit from play therapy. Unfortunately, carrying on the conversation, and delivering my message about psychological help, proved difficult. The problem was getting time to talk to Toni. Cathy reported that drop-offs were too rushed to chat. In the afternoon Miss D. was now picked up by a babysitter. Notes home went unanswered, and I grew impatient. I tried to temper this feeling with a sensitivity to Toni's life as a single mother. The pressures of a high-powered academic program, chronic money woes, and the emotional demands of parenting two young children left Toni with little time or psychic energy to address Miss D.'s needs. She later explained to me, "It's not so much that Dennis (Miss D.'s father) doesn't send the money he's supposed to. It's that there is no one to share the emotional burden of parenting with. I have to make all the decisions myself."

Finally, a second conference was scheduled. Toni arrived looking harried, and immediately announced that a taxi was picking her up to take her to the airport in ten minutes. Given the time constraint, I cut to the chase. "Toni," I began:

Someday I'd love to have a conference where we tell you all the wonderful things Denaea is doing in the classroom, and what a wonderful, caring child she is. But I'm worried about her. Cathy and I have told you that the severity of unhappiness Denaea demonstrates is unusual in our experience. You know what we are doing in the classroom, how we are ignoring the tantrums and trying to reward and encourage appropriate behavior. This isn't going to be enough. There is something deeper here. Something is underlying all this negative behavior.

Getting to the punch line, I tried to soften the blow:

> Our recommendation isn't uncommon. Over the past few years we've had a couple of kids that were in similar places, and we've found that some short-term play therapy really works wonders. Denaea is a great player, and I think she could really benefit from working out some of these issues in therapy.

I gave Toni the phone number of the local guidance center. She promised to call, and hurried off to catch her cab.

After Toni left, Cathy and I talked. I was depressed, realizing that even if Toni did follow through on our recommendation (she did) it would be months before Miss D. would see a therapist, and even longer before any results from counselling could be expected. "She'll be in kindergarten before this comes to anything, if it ever does," I groused. It was mid-November, and I was growing impatient with the situation.

One reason for my growing frustration was that Miss D.'s relation-ship with the rest of the group was deteriorating. Beyond her difficulties in-teracting positively with her peers, her incessant crying was affecting others besides me. I learned of the children's feelings at a meeting time. Unable or unwilling to stop calling out in the middle of a discussion, Miss D. had been sent away from the group. This censor produced the usual tears, and her screams of "I want my mommy" coming from the block area were clearly distracting the other children as we continued on. Deciding to face the issue, I told the group, "I'm sure you've noticed Denaea often has a hard time at meeting. Cathy and I are working to help her, but it may take a long time until she's able to say what she needs without crying." I then invited the children to express their feelings about the situation. Jack's response captured the opin-ions of his peers. He explained, "It really gets on my nerves when Denaea cries like that."

Determined to find creative strategies to help Miss D. in the classroom, I sought the help of my good friend, educator Anne Kornblatt. It was Anne who convinced me of the importance of initiating a frank discussion with the children concerning their feelings about Miss D. It was also Anne who came up with the idea for a playdough party.

Miss D. loved playdough. Whenever playdough was available, she was there. Because the other children's interest in this very tactile activity had waned as they grew older, Miss D. was often alone with the playdough. She didn't seem to mind as she happily went about making birthday cakes for herself, her mom, and occasionally for me.

I joined Miss D. at the playdough table when I could. Whenever I arrived Miss D. would immediately assign me a dramatic play part, usually infantile. "I'm the mom," she would tell me, "and you're the baby from my tummy." If I tried to assume another character, Miss D. would become insistent; I was to be the baby. In her maternal role Miss D. was alternatingly benevolent and withholding. She showered me with pretend gifts, then took them back because of some imaginary infraction. She baked me cookies, then wouldn't allow me to eat them. There seemed to be something deeply satisfying about this play for Miss D., and despite the controlling aspect, it gave us the opportunity to have positive interactions. I dubbed our sessions "playdough therapy."

Anne's thinking about the playdough party was to use this activity Miss D. loved to achieve two goals: to provide an incentive for Miss D. to use appropriate behavior, and to give Miss D. something tangible she could share with her classmates. I decided to focus on meeting times, where Miss D.'s attendance was far below 50 percent. I explained to Miss D., then to the group as a whole, the premise of the party: after Miss D. made it through twelve meetings the class would have a playdough party. To keep track of progress, and provide intermediate rewards, I would give Miss D. a popsicle stick with a sticker affixed on the top after each successful meeting. She would then place the stick into one of twelve slots cut in the bottom of an egg carton.

I encouraged her classmates to help Miss D. out both at meeting times and throughout the day. Nice words and kindness were discussed. The children were very supportive of Miss D.'s task, applauding each successful effort. Michael encouraged me to tell the parents about the party so they could help out as well. The group became very invested in the upcoming celebration.

Despite support, movement toward the party was agonizingly slow. After the first week, only two slots in the egg carton were filled. I lowered my expectations for behavior, no longer requiring that Miss D. pay attention at meeting time, asking only that she not seriously disrupt the proceedings. Still, after three weeks only half the spaces in the egg carton were filled. Time was becoming a concern. In mid-December Miss D. was scheduled to visit her family in Texas during her mother's winter vacation. At the current rate, there would be no playdough party.

Fortunately, Miss D. had a more successful fourth week. By the middle of the fifth week Miss D. had eleven slots filled. Two days before her departure, only one more victory was required.

Though she fidgeted and needed several reminders about appropriate behavior, Miss D. made it though the next meeting. I announced her triumph, and handed Miss D. the victory popsicle stick. As she proudly stuck it into the egg carton, the children yelled out, "Good job, Denaea!" After Maddy called to her, "High five!" Miss D. skipped over to receive a hand slap. She then circled the group in a spontaneous victory lap, receiving high fives from each child. Miss D. beamed as the children chatted excitedly about the impending playdough party, scheduled for the end of the day.

At exploration time Miss D. assisted the parent helper in making a fresh batch of playdough. Miss D. helped mix the ingredients and selected the color. To increase the festive mood, Miss D. then helped make some popcorn. With the accoutrements prepared, I gathered the children together at the end of the day. I told them how proud I was of Miss D. and how proud I was of them for helping out. I gave Miss D. a hug. Miss D. then announced that she had made popcorn. Amid a chorus of thank-yous, she passed out the treat to her friends. The children then adjourned for playdough. Miss D. sat at the head of the table, quietly working with the dough, basking in the good feelings of her peers.

The next day I arrived at day care hoping to build on the positive feelings of the playdough party, and to send Miss D. off on vacation in an upbeat manner. These hopes were quickly dashed. Entering the preschool room, I immediately sought Miss D. out. She greeted me warmly, and I invited her to sit on my lap. We sat together for ten minutes, laughing and chatting as the children around us played with Legos. The mood changed dramatically when cleanup time was announced. Miss D. was enraged that she hadn't had a chance to play with the Legos. I calmly informed her that I'd make a time later in the day where she could do so. Unimpressed by this offer, Miss D. swung at me. Though her punch failed to land, I felt it imperative to remove her from the group, and sat her in a chair. Rather than using this as an opportunity to cool down, Miss D. took the chair and slammed it on the ground. Then, with a mischievous glint in her eye, she tried to run out of the room. When Cathy stopped her at the door, a screaming fit ensued.

The rest of the day was a horror show. At snack time Miss D. petitioned to sit next to me. I agreed, but she then insisted on sitting on my lap, a request she knew was impossible. After I patiently explained she would have to sit in a chair, Miss D. stomped off to the block area in anger. When she returned to snack a few minutes later, I offered Miss D. the seat I had saved next to mine. She became upset, complaining that she didn't want to sit near the child seated on the other side of the chair. After I explained alternate seating was impossible, she huffed off again. She eventually returned, but then the snack itself was a problem. Finding the selection unacceptable, Miss D. threw her plate on the floor. At this point, she finally expressed what was on her mind, screaming, "I miss my mommy." Somehow, we made it through the remainder of the day, and Miss D. was off.

# Winter Breakdown

Miss D. was away for a month. During her absence a tranquility settled over the classroom. We were able to explore some compelling curriculum. It was during Miss D.'s vacation that we studied astronomy. As the date for her return neared, some parents began voicing anxiety. Would Miss D. disrupt the classroom's calm? Would we still be able to proceed with such stimulating curriculum? Did Cathy and I have a plan to better work with Miss D.? I felt protective of Miss D. and wanted to avoid her being scapegoated. I insisted to these parents that their worries were unfounded. Still, I had to admit (though of course only to Cathy) that this had been a nice break. Without Miss D. around I had more energy to devote to curriculum. Moreover, the calm in the nap room was allowing everyone peaceful rests.

As I reflected on the long fall, it was clear there was something about Miss D. we weren't reaching. This was an issue that went to the core of who Miss D. was, a result of her sense of self and her perception of the world. The profound regression observed wasn't going to be cured by stickers or even playdough parties. The negative behavior wasn't going to be extinguished by ignoring it. I remembered Miss D.'s pitiful cries, and felt that what she needed was a tremendous amount of love; what might really help would be to pick her up and rock her like a baby. This could be the key to forming a more secure, trusting relationship with Miss D. "Yeah right," my internal debate continued, now with a sarcastic tone, "That's just what she needs to help her act her age." In the end, I was still not prepared to think beyond reinforcements and rewards. I was not yet prepared to follow my intuition and try a new approach.

Miss D. returned to day care after five weeks away. She had first been with her mother's family in Texas (Toni was in South Africa doing research), and then with her father in Tennessee. The first few days back in Cambridge mirrored the beginning of the year, dreamlike in their placidity. Miss D. was attentive at meetings, transitioned easily between activities, and played cooperatively with her peers.

Then disaster struck, in the form of a tantrum at nap time. At first I reiterated the message of the last four months, "I'd love to rub your back and be with you. When you stop crying I'll come over." But the crying didn't stop, and my tension mounted. Again, the child I was responsible for was keeping everyone awake. As I sat listening to the wailing I thought, "I don't want to go back to wearing earplugs. I can't deal with six more months of these screams." I was angry; angry that my ears were hurting and angry that children I cared for deeply were again suffering because of Miss D.'s infantile behavior.

After ten minutes I hit the wall. In desperation I tried a new plan—my behavioral approach's last stand. It was a mild winter day. I dressed Miss D.

and brought her outside. I wanted to make it clear such tantrums were not acceptable. I wanted there to be a large, negative consequence for such behavior. I told Miss D. that when she stopped crying I would take her inside. Until then, I would make sure she was safe, but I wasn't going to be with her. Quiet did not come quickly. Miss D. was outside for thirty minutes. The next day she stayed outside forty-five minutes. She certainly was receiving negative feedback for her behavior. It just was that the feedback didn't seem to be working.

Cathy and I talked that evening. She gently expressed her concern about my being so punitive. I knew she was right. My new plan was a failure. But that left open the question of what to do instead. Desperate times demand desperate measures, and these were desperate times. I tentatively voiced my emerging thoughts about how Miss D.'s behaviors were the result of deep-seated emotional needs, and that forming trusting relationships was the key to turning the situation around. I explained how I thought we needed to respond to Miss D. not as a preschooler, but as a younger child in order to form these relationships. Then I held my breath. To my relief, Cathy was excited by the analysis. We proceeded to formulate an approach that proved surprisingly successful.

## Hope Springs Eternal

The next day I arrived at work with a rocking chair. Before nap, instead of sitting with the group to hear a story, Miss D. sat in my lap as I read her *Good Night Moon*. We had begun what I wistfully call Attachment Therapy.

I took the name Attachment Therapy from Attachment Theory, a psychological paradigm concerned with explaining children's social and emotional development. I am going to describe the theory in some detail because it helped me figure out how to work with Miss D. However, I want to emphasize that someone else could have formulated a plan similar to Cathy's and mine without reference to any academic theory.

I first heard of Attachment Theory in a graduate seminar at Tufts University taught by Ann Easterbrooks. When Professor Easterbrooks explained the first major premise of the theory, that children are genetically programmed to seek the proximity of their caregivers, I flashed onto a film about Konrad Lorenz that I had seen as a undergraduate. The film showed Lorenz, a pioneer in the field of animal behavior and instincts (ethology), investigating "imprinting" behavior in geese. Lorenz imprinted a brood of goslings onto himself. The film showed Lorenz walking in his garden, followed faithfully by a dozen or so goslings. There were shots of Lorenz swimming in a pond, followed by his goslings. Next were shots of Lorenz rowing a boat, followed by his goslings.

As a teacher, there have been times when I have fancied myself as Lorenz, walking along with a dozen or more children "imprinted" on me. These moments of attachment are very rewarding, and my work in the classroom convinced me of the importance of solid child-teacher bonds. Which is why, as I began learning about it, Attachment Theory made so much sense to me.

I soon found my connection between Lorenz and Attachment Theory was not coincidental. John Bowlby, a British psychiatrist and the intellectual father of Attachment Theory, was heavily influenced by the ethological perspective. Bowlby believed there was an evolutionary basis for children's attachment behaviors; attachment behaviors helped protect children from danger while facilitating safe exploration of the environment in the long period of childhood dependency. Children who stayed near enough protective adults to be safe, while exploring enough to learn the skills necessary for adulthood, had a better chance of survival and passed these traits on to their offspring.

Bowlby described attachment behaviors, noting how they change as children mature. The first six months of life is a time of "pre-attachment" behaviors. Infants smile and coo (eliciting attention from caregivers), and cry when distressed, but these behaviors are not integrated into a coherent system organized around any particular person. During the second six months of life (coinciding with the onset of locomotion), children's attachment behaviors become organized and focused on a small number of people. These older infants signal alarm over the presence of unfamiliar adults, and mobile infants seek the proximity of an "attachment figure" when threats are perceived. During toddlerhood, the role attachment takes is complicated by other emerging psychological issues such as the search for autonomy. Nevertheless, attachment behaviors continue. Stress (e.g., fatigue, illness, unfamiliar situations and settings) continues to activate the attachment system, producing toddler attachment behaviors (crying, clinginess). A sense of security is still provided largely through physical proximity to an attachment figure. With security satisfied, toddlers actively explore the environment. Preschoolers' increased cognitive and communicative abilities again change the operation of the attachment system. Attachment relationships begin to move into a more abstract context where physical proximity is no longer the major goal of the child. A sense of security can be reached, for a limited time, through mental representations of attachment figures. In other words, preschoolers can visualize important people in their lives, and achieve some comfort by thinking about them.

Of course, children's attachment behaviors take place with partners. Bowlby believed that, like children, these adult partners are genetically programmed for their roles; roles which include holding, feeding, and in general, comforting the children they are attached to. But all attachment relationships are not equal. For a variety of physical, social, and psychological reasons there is a wide range in how effective attachment figures are in providing children physical and emotional sustenance.

The psychological implications of the quality of children's attachment relationships is the second major pillar of Attachment Theory. For Bowlby, insight into the emotional importance of attachment came from his work in the orphanages of postwar Europe. In these institutions Bowlby observed infants who received little more than custodial care from their overworked caretakers. While these babies cried less over time, they also became sullen and withdrawn. Despite the fact that their physical needs were met, these children grew up with serious emotional problems. From these observations Bowlby argued that the quality of attachments children form directly impact their later mental health, taking the Freudian position that early relationships shape emotional development.

Bowlby believed that children's sense of self emerges within the context of their attachment relationships. In simplified terms, children come to see themselves as they are treated. In the 1960s Bowlby's colleague, Canadian psychologist Mary Ainsworth, provided important empirical support for this position that children's emerging sense of self is shaped by the quality of their early attachment relationships. Through a decade of research, Ainsworth learned to reliably classify children as securely or insecurely attached to their caregivers, explain how these qualities of attachments develop, and detail the implications for children's self-esteem. *Securely* attached children have experienced caregiving where their needs were met in a predictable and loving manner. Such children construct an understanding of caregivers as loving and rational. Concurrently, they construct a complementary sense of self as worthy of love. *Insecurely* attached children experience caregiving that fails to meet their needs in a reliable manner. With needs unmet, these children construct an understanding of caregivers as unavailable or unpredictable. Concurrently, they come to view themselves as unworthy or incompetent, though this sense of self is often masked behind a facade of defensiveness. In the psychiatric community, there is the belief that significant life events can alter these perceptions. However, once a child's understanding of the world is set, he or she interprets events through a lens of security or defensiveness, making the sense of self resistant to change.

Bowlby and Ainsworth were products of their time. Their work focused almost exclusively on the relations between children and their mothers. As times changed, so did Attachment Theory. In the 1970s, researchers began to study children and their fathers. In the 1980s, attachment relationships with "secondary" attachment figures (e.g., grandparents, aunts, uncles, siblings, and day care teachers) were considered. That children have multiple attachment relationships is not surprising given the evolutionary advantage to having such relationships with more than one adult. The research on secondary attachments has led to some interesting conclusions. First, it seems that children maintain separate models or understandings for each attachment figure. Children can be securely attached to their parents and insecurely attached to their day care teacher or vice versa. But despite their independence, children's understandings of relationships influence one another. Children bring their histories along when building new relationships. For example, those securely attached to their mothers bring a sense of trust to new relationships, and are more likely to become securely attached to their day care teachers. Conversely, children who are insecurely attached to their mothers bring a sense of mistrust to new relationships, and it is much harder for teachers to form secure relationships with these children.

All of this is a long way of explaining why there was a rocking chair in my preschool classroom. My analysis was that at the root of Miss D.'s behavior was the question of attachment. My sense was that Miss D. was insecurely attached to her mother. Miss D.'s difficult temperament as an infant, and her mother's demanding schedule, certainly could have resulted in such an outcome. Miss D.'s clinginess at home and defensiveness at day care fit the profile of a child with insecure attachments. Miss D. seemed to be replicating insecure attachments with Cathy and me, explaining the unpredictable and volatile nature of her interactions with us. Such a diagnosis would also explain why traditional limit setting was not working. Effective limits are set within the context of trusting relationships. Here, limits are ultimately felt by the child as supportive. There was a serious lack of trust in Miss D.'s relationship with her teachers. She experienced our limit setting as punitive, and was stuck in a self-perpetuating negative pattern of behavior.

Our goal was to change the nature of these relationships, forming secure attachments with Miss D. Given the conservative nature of children's perceptions, this was going to take some work. Here, any help academia could provide came to an end. Neither Bowlby, Ainsworth, or any subsequent Attachment Theorist had written about how to form secure secondary attachments with children insecurely attached to their primary caregivers. Despite a lack of guidance, Cathy and I knew something very different had to be tried. We decided that the something different was to treat Miss D. as a younger child; to comfort and coddle her like an infant or toddler. The idea was to go back and start again, employing techniques used to begin secure attachments. To start over, we developed a three-pronged plan.

First, we reconfigured Miss D.'s transition to nap. Instead of being with the group at story time (where she had difficulty attending, often starting a downward spiral of interactions which culminated in a screaming fit on her mat), she would read with Cathy or me in the rocking chair. This institutionalized a time during the day for physical closeness and positive interaction, and would hopefully relax her in preparation for sleep. Second, we completely changed our strategy regarding tantrums. Instead of isolating and ignoring, we decided to embrace and coddle, picking her up in much the same way one would a crying infant. Third, we temporarily abandoned our quest to have Miss D. master meeting time etiquette. Realizing that she was not yet up for the task, we decided to have Miss D. assist the parent helper prepare snack, joining meetings at the end when she could hopefully sit through the final minutes of the activity.

Over the next days, weeks, and months I rocked Miss D. before nap. Our sessions were not without struggles. Some days Miss D. would procrastinate in getting started; other days, leaving the rocker was difficult. But despite these bumps, our time together was very positive. For our initial rocking sessions I brought in two books my sons enjoyed as toddlers, Margaret Wise Brown's *Good Night Moon* and *Runaway Bunny*. I assumed we would soon move on to books for older children, but Miss D. was enamored with these titles. She was taken by the baby bunny that ran from its mother, and the mother rabbit that single-mindedly pursued its baby. She enjoyed the fact that similar characters populated both books. Overall, our time in the rocker seemed to relax Miss D. She would come to her mat without much fuss, and easily fall asleep.

It was the second part of the plan, holding Miss D. when she was upset, that wrought a magical transformation. The first time I picked Miss D. up when she was crying seemed to shock her; this was not the response she expected. But within seconds she relaxed and stopped crying. I put her down about a minute later. Very quickly Miss D. grew accustomed to this response. She continued to cry, but the duration of such episodes was cut in half. While holding her I would tell Miss D. that she didn't have to cry for me to pick her up, that she could just ask to be held. But the message that really mattered was the nonverbal one, that I was going take care of her even when she was crying, even when she was upset and angry. This was the message Miss D. desperately needed to hear.

While I felt funny rocking a four-year-old in my arms, there was no denying the strategy was having a significant impact. In February, tantruming was no longer a daily occurrence. By March, a week could go by without a major incident. By April, Miss D. was a different person in the classroom. This was not to say life with her was smooth sailing, but the level of disturbance had been taken down a notch. When Miss D. would have tantrumed, she now cried. When she would have cried, she now complained. When she would have complained, she now quietly complied.

Even through traumatic life events, Miss D. remained intact. In mid-April, Toni, burnt out from schoolwork, took a solo vacation. Coincidentally, Miss D.'s father came for an unprecedented visit. Dad's stay began the day Toni left, but lasted only through the weekend. For the remaining five days of her mom's trip, Miss D. was cared for by a sitter. Such an occurrence would be traumatic for any preschooler. For this particular child it seemed like a recipe for disaster. Amazingly, Miss D. sailed through the week at day care.

Her behavior less volatile, Miss D. began making social inroads. The other children appreciated the decrease in tantrums. Michael told Max, "Let's not call her crybaby anymore." Miss D.'s overtures for play were increasingly accepted, and children began inviting her into their games. Miss D. was getting along with all the children in the group, with one notable exception—Joy.

Miss D. and Joy were the only two African American girls in the class. Their similarities ended with their skin color. Where Miss D. was thin, Joy was stout. Where Miss D. was outgoing, Joy was shy. Where Miss D. was an outsider in the group, Joy was an integral class member. Fate had thrown them together. As single moms, Toni and Joy's mothers became friends. Joy's mom regularly drove Miss D. home after day care, depriving Joy of precious time alone with her mother. Joy hated Miss D., and Miss D. took delight in tormenting Joy.

Joy never met her dad. As an important male in her life, I served as a father figure. At times, it was difficult for Joy to share me with the other children. The sight of me rocking with her nemesis, Miss D., was a bitter pill for Joy to swallow. Over time, her displeasure rose to the boiling point. One day at nap, as Miss D. lay quietly, Joy began tantruming. It was as if a demon had left Miss D.'s body and entered Joy's. The next day Joy took another unprovoked fit. After she calmed down we talked. She confirmed my intuition about what was on her mind:

*Ben:* It seems like something is bothering you.

*Joy:* [no response]

*Ben:* If you can tell me what's up maybe I can do something about it. And a lot of times just telling someone what's wrong can help you feel better.

*Joy:* [no response]

*Ben:* I might be wrong here, but I have the feeling this has to do with Denaea and the rocking chair. Is that right?

*Joy [in a quiet voice]:* Yeah.

*Ben:* Are you mad that Denaea gets to rock with me?

*Joy:* Yeah.

*Ben:* Would you like a turn to rock with me?

*Joy:* Yeah!!

As a result of our chat, I promised Joy I would try to make a time each day to rock with her.

While this might have opened a flood gate of requests, I was pretty sure my offer to Joy would not result in my spending the entire day in the rocking chair. I was right. While a few children were curious about the rocking chair, one turn satisfied them. They were more interested in playing with their friends than sitting in my lap. Everyone in the group accepted that now Joy and Miss D. needed to be rocked. With the exception of Miss D.

Miss D. was green with envy, and she did not express her jealousy appropriately. One day before nap time, as I sat in the rocker with Joy, she took a stack of books, threw them on the floor, and screamed. When Miss D. awoke from nap that day, the rocking chair was gone. I had removed it from the room. When she noticed its absence I explained, "I had to take the rocking chair away. It was causing too much trouble. I know you get jealous when Joy is in the rocking chair, but it's my job to take care of her, just like I take care of you. I want to bring the rocking chair back because I really like sitting and reading to you, but there can't be any more screaming fits about it." To my delight, a rational conversation ensued. Miss D. acknowledged her jealousy, and promised to refrain from further incidents. The rocker returned to the room.

Miss D. knew she had made important progress, as evidenced at the end of one meeting time in May. Michael, who was calling the group to snack that day, selected Miss D. last. Back in the winter or fall, this would have proved disastrous. But on this spring day, Miss D. went off nonchalantly to wash her hands. Later she told me, "I was called last, but I didn't cry. I'm getting big. Soon I can go to a big kids school."

## Into the Summer Sunset

At the end of May, Toni completed her graduate program and began preparations to move her family back to Texas. Her plan was to step off the professional fast track for a year, and focus on her children. The move was set for mid-June.

No doubt in anticipation of this upcoming transition, the first day of June brought an unwelcome surprise. At nap time Miss D. unexpectedly burst into tears. While I was eventually able to soothe her to sleep, the source of her concern had to be addressed. When she awoke from nap I began:

> I know you are worried about your last day. That isn't for three more weeks. That's a lot of days that we still have together in day care. After we say good-bye I'll write you letters. And of course, your mom and your family will always be with you in Texas to take care of you.

Despite my chat, I was certain that the move, and the separation it represented, would produce a great deal of anxiety. I braced for the upcoming storm.

The storm never hit. Miss D.'s last few weeks at day care were good by anyone's standard. The bottom line was she acted like a four-year-old. She played happily with her peers. She accepted limits. While she still loved the rocking chair, it seemed an almost sentimental attachment.

Then it was Miss D.'s last day. This was the day that during my winter breakdown I fantasized about. But so much had changed. We had gone from earplugs to hugs. I was very sad to say good-bye. Her peers also seemed sad that she was leaving. At meeting time we bid Miss D. a formal farewell. Maddy's good-bye was typical, telling her friend, "We liked it when you didn't whine and cry in the nap room. Then we liked playing with you." Miss D.'s response was heartfelt, "I'm going to miss you guys when I go to Texas." After the meeting Toni came to take her daughter, and Miss D. and I said a personal good-bye. She told me, "Ben, you're a very nice teacher and I want to give you a present." The present was a painting of a rainbow, and a hug. With that, Miss D. was off.

## Jason's Story

For the past few years I have taught a course entitled "Developmental Learning" at Lesley College. Each semester I tell my students, preservice and inservice teachers beginning a masters program in education, about my experiences with Miss D. Without fail, a significant number of them relate strongly to the story, recognizing in Miss D. a child they have taught.

Some of these students tell me how the story has inspired them to try a new approach with a particular child in their class. Over the weeks they report how they are providing more hugs and attention in an attempt to forge stronger relationships with these children. For the most part, these efforts fizzle out by the end of the semester, and I hear about a return to reward systems and sticker charts.

Clearly part of the reason these experiments fail is the pressures of class size. With a group of up to thirty children it is extraordinarily difficult to provide the attention necessary to form a secure bond with a child like Miss D. Teachers revert to more time-efficient strategies to try to manage such children's behaviors. But I think something else is at work here as well, that is, a behavioral approach to children's emotions is so deeply rooted in our culture that teachers naturally revert to this mode of operation. Breaking away from a mind-set of reinforcements and rewards takes focus and perseverance.

I write this with a certain amount of humility, being guilty of this default to behavioralism in my own teaching. The year after I worked with Miss D. I had a little boy named Jason in my class. Jason was energetic, athletic, and adorable—and filled with anger. His verbal and physical aggressiveness toward his peers sabotaged his strong desire for friendships. Cathy and I worked hard to help Jason control his aggressive impulses and interact appropriately with his classmates. We had mild success.

At home, Jason often stayed up very late. He arrived at day care very early. By lunch time he was exhausted, which aggravated his negative behaviors.

It was essential for him to nap. I was told by his Stomper Room teachers that he often had difficulties settling down for rest, but holding him generally brought about sleep.

Armed with this information, I began the year by allowing Jason to rest on his own. I reasoned I would give him the opportunity to get to sleep independently. On the days he was unable to settle himself, I would pick him up and rock him to sleep.

For the first month, naps alternated between Jason falling asleep on his mat and in my arms. On the days I had to pick him up Jason gave mute protests. I told him, "Today you were too fidgety, but tomorrow you can try again to go to sleep by yourself." I reasoned that, given Jason's professed desire to be on his mat and the consequences of fooling around, he would move to more independent naps over time.

In fact, the opposite ensued. Jason became more boisterous at nap time, causing me to pick him up with greater frequency, causing him to protest even louder about being held. I had little sympathy, and responded to the protests directly, explaining that he was being held as a direct consequence of his behavior. Jason answered these explanations with increasing anger. One day, after I picked him up following some particularly disruptive behavior, Jason yelled, "I hate you!" and spit in my face.

We had fallen into a downward spiral. I realized my behavioral-based strategy for Jason's nap wasn't working. To break the cycle, I tried a new approach the next day. Instead of waiting for Jason to misbehave at nap time, I picked him up immediately, explaining, "I'm going to rock you now because I love you. You'll go to sleep and get the energy you need to have a good afternoon." Jason protested briefly. I ignored the outburst, gently rocked him, and soon he was fast asleep. The next day there were no protests, and again, Jason fell quickly asleep.

Holding Jason at nap time was not a miracle cure. His anger, which I believe stemmed from attachment issues, still manifested itself in aggression. But we no longer fought each other at nap, so our relationship grew stronger and I was better able to help him deal with his aggressive impulses. Nap time, needless to say, was 100 percent improved. I had relearned the lessons of Miss D.

## Resources

The seminal work on Attachment Theory is John Bowlby's three-volume set *Attachment and Loss* (New York: Basic Books, 1969). For those looking for something a bit shorter and less technical than Bowlby's thousand-page opus, I recommend Robert Karen's piece "Becoming Attached" in the February

1990 *Atlantic Monthly*, pp. 35–70. Karen does a nice job explaining both the theory and the intellectual history of the paradigm.

My research has found a dearth of writing on how attachment theory informs teachers' efforts to work with "difficult" children. My two previous ventures into this area, "A Practitioner's Perspective on the Implication of Attachment Theory for Daycare Professionals" (1992, *Child Study Journal*, 22(3), 201–32), and "How Understanding Attachment Theory Can Help Make Us Better Teachers" (1994, *NHSA Journal*, 12(4), 39–47) look at methods of fostering child-teacher bonds. However, both articles sidestep the question of how to achieve secure relations with children like Miss D.

Another theoretical perspective that provides insights into the case of Miss D. is Erik Erikson's (1950) "Eight Stages of Man." Erikson maintains there are eight pivotal emotional conflicts that come to the fore during particular points in the life cycle. The path to emotional health, according to Erikson, is paved by creative solutions to these conflicts. The emotional conflict faced by infants is trust versus mistrust. New to the world, the child learns whether or not its needs will be met, and if the world is a relatively safe place. Ideally, the infant comes to trust others and begins to trust itself. If a child does not develop a sense that the world is a safe place, a sense of mistrust develops and carries into later life. I believe the latter was the case with Miss D. At the beginning of the year it seemed like every day Miss D.'s actions asked, "Am I safe here? Will you take care of me? Will you take care of me even when I scream?" Only after her questions were answered affirmatively could Miss D. move beyond her infantile behavior.

In some ways, Erikson's theory provides a more satisfying explanation of Miss D. than does Attachment Theory. Erikson describes a continuum of trust versus mistrust while Attachment Theory presents a binary model (secure/insecure) where you either are secure or you aren't. Despite obvious issues, Miss D. is a little girl with a special spark. Before she graduated to the Preschool Room her Stomper Room teacher, Aren Stone, told me, "She's the kind of kid who takes a tremendous amount, but in the end gives a tremendous amount back." It took me a long time to see any reciprocity in our relationship, but in the end I certainly did. Miss D.'s ability to give back speaks to something she obtained in her relationship with her mother. That something had to be drawn out, but it must have been there all along.

Miss D.'s favorite rocking chair books, *Good Night Moon* and *Runaway Bunny*, were first published in the 1940s. Written by Margaret Wise Brown and illustrated by Clement Hurd, these classics are currently available in a variety of formats, hard cover, paperback, and board book, from Harper Collins (New York).

My day care center's secret playdough recipe, guaranteed to remain fresh for weeks if stored in an air tight container, is:

    2 cups flour
    1 cup salt
    1/4 cup oil
    3 teaspoons cream of tarter
    2 cups water (approximately)
    2 tablespoons food coloring

Mix in a medium pot. Cook over medium heat for three to five minutes, stirring often.

I want to thank my friend Anne Kornblatt for her creative ideas in working with Miss D. and her patient listening as I struggled through my long fall and winter breakdown. Thanks and appreciation as well to my co-teacher, Cathy Craddock, for her support and wisdom in working with Miss D. My experience here confirms the tremendous value of having a partner in the classroom. Finally, I want to express my gratitude to Miss D. and her mother, Toni. Their courage, determination, and honesty taught me a great deal.

# 5

―

# *In Search of Fairness: South Africa*

## Nelson and Me

On June 23, 1990, at 11:52 A.M. something remarkable occurred in the history of Boston broadcasting. For three minutes and twenty-five seconds almost every radio station in town played the same song: "Nkosi Sikelel Afrika" ("God Bless Africa"). The music most closely associated with the struggle for freedom and justice in South Africa was on the air that bright summer morning to mark an extraordinary event in the history of my city. On June 23, 1990, at 11:52 A.M., a plane carrying Nelson Mandela landed at Logan International Airport. Chills ran down my spine as I listened to the radio, knowing he had arrived.

I first heard of Nelson Mandela and the antiapartheid movement he led a dozen years earlier as a freshman in college. I had wandered into a meeting of social activists calling for the university to divest its financial holdings in South Africa. What I heard that evening stirred something deep in my eighteen-year-old soul. I was shocked to learn how the majority Blacks were treated as slaves in their own land. Deprived of basic political rights, they were forced into subsistence existences for the benefit of a wealthy White elite. Those who resisted were imprisoned, tortured, and even murdered by the authorities. After the meeting I read more about the issue. I learned how, during the eighteenth and nineteenth centuries, Dutch and British settlers appropriated land from the Khoikhoi, Xhosa, and Sans people, who historically had lived on the southern tip of Africa. I learned about the apartheid system and its repressive laws, which placed South Africans into one of four racial categories—White, Black, Colored, or Mixed—and then excluded non-Whites from virtually all the power and wealth of the country. I was saddened to read that the most repressive laws went into effect after World War II, a time when the rest of the world was reacting to the horrors of Nazism and becoming more progressive on issues of race. Then I learned of the African National Congress' courageous struggle to end apartheid and read of the movement's valiant leader, Nelson Mandela, who was imprisoned since 1962.

Back in the late 1970s, the repression in South Africa, like that in Eastern Europe, seemed to be a permanent fixture on the world scene. There were protest marches, letter-writing campaigns, and product boycotts, but apartheid continued and Nelson Mandela remained in prison. Then, in the late 1980s, the status quo was shaken worldwide. The Berlin Wall crumbled. A "Velvet Revolution" swept Czechoslovakia. And on February 10, 1990, after more than ten thousand days in prison, Nelson Mandela gained his freedom.

I was elated, and my enthusiasm bubbled over into the classroom. While I normally never mentioned current events to my preschoolers, the day after Mandela's release I brought in his photograph from the front page of the newspaper and told my students about this historic event. Four months later with a hundred thousand others, I welcomed Mr. Mandela to Boston.

## Why South Africa?

The depth of my feelings about the struggle in South Africa and Nelson Mandela's visit to Boston certainly reveals something about me. But this admission of political idealism should not come as a surprise; with salaries for day care teachers hovering just above the minimum wage, it is obvious that people pursuing careers in early childhood education do so for love, not money. For many of us, this love involves a special kind of political activism: we work with children to build a better future.

Building a better future involves raising children to be citizens, not consumers or couch potatoes. It means raising children to be thoughtful, compassionate, and responsible, and to have values. It means raising children to be active in their communities and the world at large.

Getting off my soap box, and back to the realities of the classroom, I must admit that after fifteen years of teaching, I am humbled by the question of how to raise such children. To start, what values do we highlight? Responsibility? Compassion? Perseverance? Honesty? Integrity? Respect? Tolerance? Of course, all are important, but teaching involves making choices. Choosing here also involves deciding the contexts in which values will be taught, since young children can not comprehend these issues in the abstract. For example, should tolerance be presented in the context of race, religion, ethnicity, gender, sexual orientation, or physical ability? So many pressing moral questions make prioritizing a daunting task.

And that's the easy part. Teachers must then confront the question of how children learn these values. The trick here is knowing that indoctrination doesn't work. We adults can lecture about the right way to act and think, we can even enforce codes of moral behavior through rewards and punishments. But in the end, children take our messages and interpret them through their own frames of reference and ways of thinking. They can even be reactionary, willfully defying adult pronouncements and ideas. Moreover, ultimately we want children who act morally because of an internal sense of what is right rather than out of fear of retribution.

Moral development is a complex process. Somehow, children take what they see and hear and develop moral frameworks. With young children you can see this process at work. Preschoolers tend to be junior philosophers. They wonder about God. They ponder the meaning of death. They are particularly concerned with goodness, the question of evil, and issues of fairness. Through discussions, observations, and just living life, they are actively constructing their sense of morality. I face the challenge all teachers who are committed to raising citizens have: for the short time we spend with a particular child, and while meeting our other teaching obligations, enhancing this child's moral development.

I tend to fall back on my general mode of operation with preschoolers: I try to engage them in curriculum. With children eager to consider moral issues, I want at least some of the curriculum units presented each year to engage children in ethical questions about the real world. I try to let the children guide me to the part of the world and the particular ethical questions we consider.

Direction emerges from each class' needs. By "needs" I am referring to the troublesome social dynamics and moral issues that arise each year in the classroom. Needs may involve a particular child requiring assistance integrating into the group, or perhaps girls being excluded from the block area, or children laughing when they see a person in a wheelchair. The group I'll focus on in this chapter had a series of needs raised by a girl named Denaea, a child my co-teacher Cathy and I affectionately referred to as Miss D. As explained in the preceding chapter, Miss D. was in crisis. She had frequent temper tantrums and behaved in an antisocial manner. As a result, the other children often shunned her. Patterns developed, and even Miss D.'s positive overtures were rebuked, creating more tantrums and exacerbating her outcast status. Thus, one glaring need was to help Miss D. become part of the group; another was to help the other children become more tolerant and less quick to scapegoat people who don't easily fit in. Further, the plan I developed to help Miss D. with her emotional crisis released her from certain routines the other children had to follow. For example, instead of attending meetings Miss D. would assist the parent helper to prepare snack. The other children vigorously protested what they perceived as Miss D.'s special privileges. What is fair, and whether everything has to be the same to be fair, were hotly debated issues in the classroom.

Enter South Africa. During her winter break, Miss D.'s mother traveled to South Africa. Studying this country would be a way to highlight and honor something about Miss D.'s family, hopefully making her feel more part of the class and improving her social stock with the other children. Given my interest in South Africa, I began considering a unit.

As I thought about South Africa I felt increasingly sure that it met the test for compelling preschool curriculum. There are many fascinating aspects of the country that would capture the children's attention: the nature, the music, the food, and the historical struggle against apartheid. It was in the story of the antiapartheid movement where I saw the clearest connection to the interests of these children. As a group, this class was obsessed with fairness. Cries of "that's not fair," far outnumbered the other common preschool complaints of "s/he hit me" and "that's mine." I was forced to create turn-taking lists for mundane daily events (holding my hand on walks, sitting on my lap at story time) to avoid divisive disputes. With the issue of fairness so central to the drama of modern-day South Africa, I was confident the children would find the story engaging. In turn, I hoped the story would create a context in which we could discuss questions of fairness.

The remainder of this chapter explores our study of South Africa, how stories were used to bring this distant land to life, the children's responses to learning of the antiapartheid struggle, and our discussions about fairness both in South Africa and at home. The chapter also contains musings about how children's fantasy and play can further inquiry, and a description of our partly imaginary, partly real, correspondence with Nelson Mandela.

## From Cambridge to Cape Town

It is almost 7,000 miles from Cambridge to Cape Town, a fact my class learned on the first day of our study of South Africa. After locating both cities on a world map, and noting the immense ocean between them, we turned our attention to a second map, one I had drawn for my young geographers, just of South Africa. Asking the children what they noticed about this second map highlighted some points of interest about our topic of study: nature preserves, Johannesburg (the city of gold), Cape Town, Table Mountain, and the surrounding Atlantic and Indian Oceans.

The children were curious about these features, but with the exception of Miss D., it was clear that none of them had heard of South Africa before. All this talk of distant cities, countries, mountains, and oceans was very abstract, and for them, the psychological distance between Cambridge and Cape Town was at least as great as the physical one. Bringing this faraway land to life was a prerequisite to any meaningful discussion about the politics of the country. Engaging, exciting, and interesting the children about South Africa became the agenda for week one of the curriculum.

My attempt to generate this excitement began later that Monday. In our meeting at the end of the day I announced that the preschoolers had received a letter. When I showed the envelope to the group, Max immediately recognized the Cape Hunting Dog on the stamp, and inferred that the letter was from South Africa. I confirmed his suspicions, opened the letter, and read to an expectant audience:

Dear Preschoolers,

My name is Ashraf and I live in Cape Town, South Africa. I am very interested in wild animals and hear that you are too. Would you like to visit me in South Africa? We could go on a safari to see wild animals.

Love,

Ashraf

The children enthusiastically accepted the invitation.

Thus began the epic tale of the preschoolers' trip to South Africa. My hope was that the story would bring South Africa to life for the children. While I couldn't take their bodies overseas, I could take their minds. The story also provided an overarching structure for activities on the subject. However, there was a major hurdle to overcome in telling this story; I am not South African and, despite my desire to, have never visited the country. Here I was helped by the surprisingly large number of picture books set in South Africa. This literature was the source of characters and plot lines, and provided my tale with a measure of authenticity.

For example, my choice of correspondent was not random. The children "met" Ashraf earlier that day in the book *Somewhere in Africa*. Written by Ingrid Mennen and Niki Daly and illustrated by Nicolas Maritz, *Somewhere in Africa* tells of a young boy who lives in Africa, but not, the text explains, "the Africa where lions laze in golden grass, not the Africa where crocodiles glide through muddy rivers, silent and hungry." Ashraf lives in a city "at the very tip of the great African continent." Even though he has never seen them in the wild, Ashraf is fascinated by African animals, an interest he shares with many of the preschoolers.

The next day the tale continued. Ashraf's invitation accepted, the preschoolers packed their suitcases, and after a twelve-hour plane flight, were met at the Cape Town airport. The preschoolers and their host then boarded a Land Rover, and headed off on safari to Auginbies Falls National Park in the Northern Cape.

I enacted the journey to the country with props taken from the block area. Two long blocks served as the Land Rover. Four-by-two-inch blocks affixed with the children's photos represented members of the expedition. I hoped my use of these props would inspire South African play in the block area during exploration times. Everyone on board, the naturalists drove out of Cape Town along the coastal road, then headed inland over the South African veld or plain. After a day of hard driving they arrived at a village outside of the national park, where Ashraf's friend Manyoni lived. Manyoni greeted Ashraf and the preschoolers warmly, and invited them to a dinner in their honor in the center of the village. Taken from the book *Where Are You Going Manyoni?* by Catherine Stock, Manyoni is a little girl who lives out on the veld. To reach school she must traverse some ruggedly beautiful countryside, passing by a host of wildlife. While the book is set in Zimbabwe, the landscape and rural life depicted is common to southern Africa. In my story, the preschoolers sat around a campfire eating dinner as Manyoni told them of the adventures that lay ahead of them:

> Tomorrow you will be going on a safari, and you'll see many wonderful things. Maybe you'll see an elephant. Maybe you'll see a giraffe. Maybe you'll see a cheetah. Maybe you'll see a zebra. And maybe you'll see a lion!

At that exact moment, a lion roared in the distance. The children huddled together, frightened by the noise. Manyoni reassured them:

> Don't worry about that noise because we are all together. Here in South Africa we protect each other by working together. Tomorrow you will be safe because you will be all together. If you feel a bit scared, there is a special word you can say to help you feel better. The word is *aweemawa*.

Together the preschoolers repeated the special word: *aweemawa*. I then played the song "Aweemawa" (also known as "The Lion Sleeps Tonight"). Listening to the tune, the preschoolers went to sleep under the stars, dreaming of their upcoming adventure.

While we couldn't go on an actual safari, our proximity to a zoological museum did present a wonderful opportunity to view real (if no longer living) African animals. Later that same Tuesday I announced we were heading off on our safari. We walked over to the museum where the children were able to view elephants, giraffes, cheetahs, zebras, and a lion. As they walked among

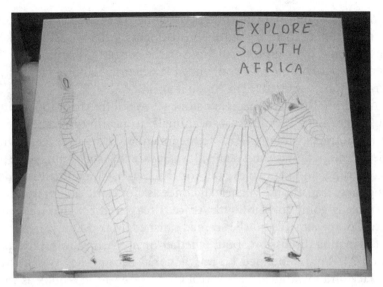

Figure 5–1. *Max's zebra, drawn at the museum*

the mounted specimens, pausing to sketch favorite species, I periodically overheard a child chant "aweemawa, aweemawa."

Leaving the museum, I let the children loose on a grass field, encouraging them to play African animals. In truth, they didn't need much encouragement. Michael and Joseph immediately became lions crawling through the grass. Miss D., Kim, and Robert raced around as cheetahs. Maddy, Max, and Jack climbed a yew bush, chattering like monkeys. Back at day care the animal play continued in a different venue. I announced that the block area, now stocked with plastic lions, zebras, elephants, and rhinos, had been rechristened a nature reserve. At exploration time the children flocked to the blocks, though the first day the reserve ended up looking more like a zoo, with walled off areas for each species. The next day I taped down some blue construction paper, and explained how animals often congregated around watering holes. The block area play that day was more "wild."

On Wednesday I continued the tale, with the preschoolers returning to Manyoni's village after an exciting day in the national park. To their surprise, the villagers had planned an evening of drumming and dancing. In real life, our student teacher Jenny Stock arranged with a friend to have a few members of an African drumming group visit the center. Instead of taking a walk that day we waited in the play yard, the adults wondering when and if the drummers would arrive. To Jenny's and my surprise, all sixteen members of the ensemble appeared. The resulting concert was the most exciting (and loudest) happening in the day care center's neighborhood in a long while. The children were enthralled, some dancing, others watching. They were especially excited when the group let them try out the instruments. After we said good-bye to the band, I gauged the group's reactions to the concert. Max thought, "It was excellent." Miss D. noted, "I really liked it when my elbows flapped [while dancing]." Robert wanted them "to do it again."

In shifting from an imaginary story set in South Africa to viewing real but no longer living South African animals, to hearing live and very loud African drummers, and then back to the imaginary story, we were navigating complex levels of fantasy and reality. I was aware that such shifts were potentially confusing, and kept an eye out for children having difficulties comprehending these transitions. Michele did once ask for clarification, wondering if we were really going to visit South Africa. I reassured her that we were only traveling "in the story," and she seemed satisfied. Max, Maddy, Jack, and Joy had a fascinating discussion about whether or not Ashraf was a real person. Max and Maddy maintained he was fictional because he "was just in the story." Jack and Joy argued he was real because he was in a book as well as a story. For the most part, the shifts between fact and fantasy were seamless. The children seemed very comfortable with the changing levels of reality.

Thursday brought the next installment of the story. After a heartfelt good-bye to Manyoni, the expedition began the trip back to Cape Town. Along the way the Land Rover stopped at the fishing village of Kalk Bay to visit Ashraf's friend Armein. The title character of *Armein's Fishing Trip* by Catherine Stock, Armein showed his new friends the village's fishing boats. Appropriating the book's main plotline, I then told how Armein, Ashraf, and the preschoolers awoke early the next morning, and stowed away on a boat heading out to sea. After a series of adventures, including saving a member of the crew who was washed overboard by a wave, the children returned safely to shore with a giant tuna they had caught.

Part six of the travelog was presented at story time at the end of the day. The preschoolers were spending the night at Armein's house. After a feast of tuna steaks and millet, they settled around Armein's mother who told them a story about Boconono, the Tom Thumb of South African lore. I learned of Boconono from *Misoso: Once upon a Time Tales from Africa*, a collection of folk tales edited by Verna Aardema. In a story I concocted for Armein's mom to tell, a magic ring needed to heal an ailing girl was lost down an ant hole. Of all the people in the village, only Boconono, because of his diminutive stature, was able to retrieve the ring.

The story continued on Friday, this installment being told right before exploration time. As motivation for an upcoming activity, I told about the preschoolers' desire to buy presents for their families back home. With the requisite rands (the South African currency) in their pockets, the children purchased some beadwork from a local shop. At the subsequent exploration time, the children had the opportunity to act out the story. Stocked with necklaces and fabrics, the house area was opened as a South African store. The store provided great bargains as the children playing the sales staff gave money away whenever a purchase was made. The currency had been produced the day before at exploration time. I used what the children dubbed "the money machine," the photocopier in the office, to produce a large number of counterfeit ten-rand notes, which the children watercolored with beautiful results. Over the next week, exploration times included the store, as well as art activities (beading, stamping on fabric) from which the store's merchandise was replenished.

The next Monday the story continued with a fond farewell to Kalk Bay and a short ride to Cape Town. Pulling up in front of Ashraf's apartment, the preschoolers were introduced to his teenage sister Maya. Standing on the sidewalk, Maya suddenly screamed, "Go hopping sideways," South African for "I'm really mad." It seemed that Maya, who was standing under an orange tree, had been hit on the head by a falling citrus. After making sure Maya was uninjured, the preschoolers began noticing the diversity of fruit trees lining the street. The story continued as:

> Ashraf pointed out an avocado tree and began climbing up its trunk. "Hold thumbs," Maya called up, which is a South African way of saying good luck. Slowly Ashraf climbed the tree until he reached a branch with some ripe avocados. He picked two for the preschoolers to try.

The group then found a pineapple tree. This time it was the preschoolers who scaled the tree and picked the fruit.

Avocados and pineapples in hand, everyone then adjourned to Ashraf and Maya's apartment where in the story, and then in real life, the preschoolers sampled these tropical fruits. Of course, avocados and pineapples could have been served at snack without the fanfare of an accompanying story, but embedding the tasting in the story connected the activity to what had become a powerful way for the children to experience South Africa.

Later that day the story continued in Ashraf's apartment. Ashraf and Maya had invited some friends over for a dance party. Again, embedded in the story was an activity, this time listening to music from South Africa. At the party, songs of Miriam Makeba, Ladysmith Black Mambazo, and Juluka played as the preschoolers danced the night away.

After six days of this epic tale the children were immersed in South Africa. They eagerly awaited the story's next installment. Their dramatic play was often set in South Africa. Some actively yearned to make an actual journey. We had traveled the 7,000 miles from Cambridge to Cape Town.

# Free Nelson!

> Sitting around the dining room table, Ashraf and the preschoolers were telling about their trip to the veld and Kalk Bay. Maya wanted to know more about the safari. Ashraf's mother asked how they caught the tuna. Everyone laughed when they remembered the orange falling on Maya's head. Then the preschoolers had a question. They had seen photographs of Maya and Ashraf's father around the apartment, but they had never met him. They wondered where he was, so they asked, "Ashraf, when is your dad coming home?" Immediately Maya, Ashraf, and their mother fell silent, the smiles gone from their faces.

We were in the second week of study. We were about to engage in curriculum where moral questions abounded. I was about to begin telling the children about the struggle for freedom in South Africa.

I thought long and hard about how to introduce this facet of South Africa. I was very comfortable telling the children about apartheid, knowing they would be right with me as I explained the unfairness of the system. What I pondered was in how much detail to present the struggle for freedom. Specifically, did I want to talk about how people were killed? Should I shield my charges from this part of the story? Would hearing of death be too much for my young students to process? In the end, I let tradition guide me. I had just attended a Passover seder where the liturgy included the story of how the ancient Egyptians attempted to murder newborn Jewish babies, and how the Almighty smote all the firstborn Egyptian males. There were no graphic accounts here, but enough details to make the story compelling. So I decided to include the fact that people were killed in my story of oppression. I knew this information would enhance the dramatic appeal of the story, and I knew this group was not naive as to the existence of death. Neither had they been so personally touched by loss that the story would be too upsetting. I continued in a hushed, somber tone:

> The room was quiet for a long time. Maya, Ashraf, and their mother looked very sad. In fact, Ashraf and his mom began to cry. Finally Maya spoke: "Our father is dead. He was killed by soldiers in the struggle to get rid of the bad laws called apartheid." The preschoolers couldn't believe what they were hearing. Ashraf's father dead? Killed by solders? Bad laws? They wanted to know more.

The preschoolers listening to my story really did want to know more. Though imaginary, Ashraf was their friend. By extension, they cared about his father. Killing by soldiers and bad laws; they were all ears. Maya continued:

> In the days of the bad laws people with dark skin weren't allowed to go to good schools, live in nice houses, have good jobs, or even vote. In fact, people with dark skin and white skin weren't allowed to go to the same day care centers, to live near each other, or even be friends.

Maya then explained how many people had worked to change the laws, her father among them. He had led meetings and marches. "One day," Maya said in a soft, sad voice, "as he was leading a march to try to end the bad laws, he was shot and killed."

The children had a very strong reaction to the story. "Like Martin Luther King," Maddy shouted out. Max wished, "That the Black people and the White people could change the laws." Jack hoped, "I could stop the bad laws and get all the Black people away from there." The children were also full of questions. Some, like "Why were soldiers allowed to do that?" did not have satisfactory answers. Others, like "What happened to the bad laws?" were addressed by the ongoing story the next day.

With the voice of Maya narrating, the children learned about the central personality of the antiapartheid movement, Nelson Mandela. Maya began by describing Mandela's childhood: how he helped with his family's flocks, and played games out on the countryside, and how his name was changed from Rolihlahla to Nelson by his English teachers when he entered school. Continuing, Maya recounted:

> When Nelson was a young man he moved to Johannesburg, the city of gold. He went to the city for adventure. What he saw there shocked him. All the gold went to the mine owners who had light skin. The miners, who had dark skin, worked very hard, but got none of the gold. They were very poor, and weren't allowed to live with their families. So the miners' children only got to see their fathers a couple of times a year. Nelson was so upset about how the miners were treated that he went to school to become a lawyer so he could work to change the laws that made life in South Africa so unfair.

Maya went on to describe to the preschoolers how Mandela joined the African National Congress, a group trying to change the bad laws. The ANC had many members, mostly Black, but some White. These people held meetings and marches, and got even more people working together to try to change the laws. Through all this effort the ANC grew very strong, and the government of South Africa got scared. So, Maya explained:

> They put Nelson Mandela, the leader of the ANC, in jail. He went to jail long before you or I were born. My mom was just a young girl when it happened. The government kept Nelson in jail for many years. Nelson's friends kept working to get rid of the bad laws, and to get Nelson out of jail. There

were meetings and marches and people wrote letters saying how important it was for Nelson to go free. Sometimes it seemed like things would never get better, but then, after spending 10,000 days in prison, Nelson Mandela was freed. He got to see his family and friends, and go all around South Africa and the world. Working with others he got rid of the bad laws. Then we had an election in South Africa where for the first time everyone, Black and White, got to vote. After all the votes were counted, you know the person who won and is now president of South Africa? It's Nelson Mandela!

I loved saying that last line, and loved the reactions of my students to this happy ending. I was grateful to be telling a story about a fight against oppression with such an unambiguously positive conclusion. For years I have told my class the story of Dr. Martin Luther King, and will continue to do so because Dr. King is an important person for children to know about. But I've noticed that while they absorb the respect that adults give to him, no one ever wants to be Dr. King in dramatic play. No preschooler wants to be killed at the end of the story.

On the other hand, everyone wanted to be Nelson Mandela. To facilitate such dramatic play I added to our collection blocks with photographs of Winnie Mandela, Desmond Tutu, Walter Susulu, several South African soldiers, and of course President Mandela. At exploration times over the next week the block area saw jails built by soldiers, and then destroyed by the preschool freedom fighters. Somehow, despite great odds, Nelson and his comrades always emerged victorious.

Spontaneously, the fight against apartheid spilled out of the block area. Janet, Maddy, Max, James, Jack, and Michael decided that the loft was Robbins Island (where Mandela was imprisoned for many years). Janet, Maddy, and Max jailed themselves, and then demanded to be released by chanting, "Freedom! Freedom!" In support of their comrades, James, Jack, and Michael prepared protest signs that read, "Free Nelson!" Drawings and paintings of the South African flag were made and displayed around the room.

The preschoolers' trip to South Africa was drawing to an end. In the story, on the second-to-last day of the unit, Ashraf announced that he had two surprises for his friends. The first surprise took the preschoolers down to the ocean. There they rode a boat over to Robbins Island and saw the cramped cell where Nelson Mandela had spent much of his adult life. Later in the day, they went to a soccer stadium and saw Nelson Mandela speak. The audience was thrilled to imagine that they had seen the South African president. The preschoolers had a new hero, a hero whose standards for justice and equality provided them a moral compass in their own search for fairness.

# What Is Fair?

Ten years ago I met a White woman from South Africa. As we discussed politics she gave a very honest, though morally bankrupt, justification for apartheid. She explained how she, on a secretary's salary, could afford to live in a very nice apartment in Johannesburg. Because wages for Blacks were so low, as part of her lease she received daily maid service. "But that's not fair!" I cried. Dismissive of my valuation, she countered, "If you could live like that, you'd like apartheid too." But I disagree. I don't think I could, I hope I wouldn't be able to, support such blatant injustice. I hope that none of my students will be able to either.

As I've mentioned, this group of children was obsessed with fairness. They were very vocal about this process, sometimes to my chagrin. One day the children in the class next door were singing "Happy Birthday" as part of dramatic play. "Not fair, not fair," Michael, Joy, and Janet shouted. "But it's just pretend," I explained. "We don't care. It's not fair," was their response.

The question of what is fair is at times crystal clear and critically important. The injustices of the apartheid system fall into this category. At other times, the issue of fairness is murkier. Miss D.'s snack-making privilege is an example of a question with more shades of gray. Sometimes questions of fairness can be petty, like complaining about the neighboring class playing birthday party. Helping this group figure out what fairness meant, and when it was important, was part of our study of South Africa.

Coinciding with the discussion of South African politics, and continuing for the two weeks until the conclusion of the unit, I introduced a series of exercises designed to help the children think about fairness. My goal wasn't to provide rigid guidelines about the issue, but to engage children, helpfully stretching and deepening their understanding of the issue.

The first exercise created a situation where the children experienced unfairness and then reflected upon it. This exercise involved voting. From the beginning of the year the group voted about various classroom issues: where to go on walks, what to name our basketball team, and occasionally what topic to study. Our votes were free and fair, with everyone given the opportunity to participate. For the first fairness exercise there was a change. I began meeting by explaining:

> We are going to vote about what to have for snack today. There is something different about this vote. It is a vote like the ones in South Africa before they changed the bad laws when only some people could vote. In our vote today only children who are three years old can vote. If you're four or five you can't vote.

I then went around the circle, asking each child their age, and informing them if they qualified to vote. Only Joseph, Kim, and Katie were. The other ten children were disenfranchised. The children's reaction to the new system, expressed in the discussion afterward, was predictable. Those who voted were satisfied; those who could not vote were quite upset. Nonvoter Michael began:

*Michael:* It's getting me really angry.

*Ben:* Why is it making you angry?

*Michael:* It's really dumb. It's the bad laws.

*Ben:* Maddy?

*Maddy:* It felt bad because it wasn't fair.

*Ben:* Why not?

*Maddy (Crying):* 'Cause you wouldn't let us vote.

*Ben (Sympathetically):* I understand. Michele?

*Michele:* It was really dumb.

*Ben:* James?

*James (Indignantly):* Preschool teachers shouldn't do such foolish things.

*Ben:* Kim, you got to vote. Was this OK or not?

*Kim:* It was OK.

*Ben:* Joseph, how do you feel?

*Joseph (Sheepishly):* Happy.

At this point Michele began to sob. Feeling the exercise had its intended impact, I announced that there would be a new vote in which everyone could participate. The announcement was cheered. After the second vote I commented that it was now easier to imagine how people in South Africa felt when, after many, many years, they were finally allowed to vote.

The next day we repeated the exercise, revising the guidelines for participation. This time only five-year-olds could vote, enfranchising Maddy, Michael, and James. Expecting these voters to endorse the new system, I was pleasantly surprised by the discussion after this second round of voting. Maddy, who was able to vote, spoke with much conviction:

*Maddy:* It's not fair. I love the younger kids!

*Ben:* Maddy, this is interesting. You are saying this is not fair even though you got to vote.

*Maddy:* Yeah, 'cause I like the littler kids better than the big kids, and I like Michael too.

*Ben:* And Michael, you are agreeing with Maddy. Why?

*Michael:* Not fair.

*Ben:* James, I have a question for you. You got to vote this time. How do you feel about this vote?

*James:* Same as I felt the last time.

*Maddy:* Go hopping sideways!

Following Maddy's lead, the entire group began chanting "go hopping sideways." Maddy, Michael, and James had persuaded everyone that to be fair no one could be prohibited from voting.

Well, almost everyone. Joseph continued to maintain, though not very loudly, that excluding children from a vote was fine as long as he could participate. In fact, throughout the study of South Africa Joseph resisted the "right" moral messages. For example, one day I joined him in the block area. As I held the block with Nelson Mandela's picture on it, he took a soldier block and told me, "Your guy is a bad guy because he tried to change the rules. He's dying. He got shot by soldiers." During the voting exercise, Joseph was unmoved by other children's unhappiness about their exclusion. In fact, he seemed almost pleased.

The situation was particularly troubling because Joseph, a fair-skinned, blond-haired boy, had periodically made racist comments. The statements were always directed at Robert, whose family was from Nigeria. Joseph would announce, "There are no dark-skinned people allowed in the house," as an effort to exclude Robert from play. When challenged, Joseph would abdicate responsibility, pointing to the wall and shrugging, "See that sign. It says, "No dark-skinned people allowed." I would always take down these imaginary signs.

Joseph was in need of moral education, but I was unsure how to proceed. I had a strong urge to change his offensive behavior immediately, and probably could have browbeaten him into parroting the right response to the voting and apartheid questions, or at the very least silenced his dissent. But on reflection, that wasn't the way to advance his moral development. I suspected Joseph's family life, which was in turmoil, might account for his reactionary tendencies. I tried to keep in mind that racist comments from a preschooler mean something very different than such comments from adults, and tried to get Joseph to see the issue of racism and fairness from different perspectives. For example, after the voting exercise where he was excluded I told him, "This is how the people in South Africa with dark skin felt when they couldn't vote. They felt very sad. Can you feel that?" I suspected that deep down he could.

While heartened by the children's responses to the second vote, it was true they could be altruistic here without giving anything up. Voting rights could be extended without those previously enfranchised suffering any loss. To challenge the children further, I introduced a second exercise where they might have to give something up to make a situation fair.

The second exercise was entitled "The South African Fair Game." In rules gleaned from other cooperative games, I explained to Maddy, Joy, and Michael, the children who had chosen this as their exploration time activity, that:

> This is a game that you win only if you make things fair. In a minute I'm going to pass out some money. Each of you will get a different amount. You'll have to talk about how to make things fair so that everybody is happy. When everyone is happy, when everyone thinks that the amount of money they have is fair, then we'll have a celebration.

Some South African coins were then passed out. Maddy received ten, Joy three, and Michael one. Michael reacted quickly, declaring, "Its not fair!" I responded by asking the group, "How are you going to make it fair so everyone can win?"

It was intriguing watching the children negotiate their search for fairness. Maddy gave Michael and Joy each a coin, and announced, "I'm happy." But Michael and Joy weren't. After some haggling, coins changed hands again. Soon, all three children had fairly equal holdings, and they told me, "We're happy." To celebrate we made popcorn, though ironically, Michael complained that it wasn't fair that he was the last to pour the kernels in the machine.

Just then Max and James arrived, and I set up a second round of the "Fair Game." Playing with five proved more difficult for the children. I again distributed the coins unequally, and let the children negotiate. In her search for fairness, Joy gave away all her coins, then realized that this didn't feel right, and demanded some back. Max was concerned not only with the quantity of coins, but also about obtaining specific denominations. This prompted Joy to refuse the smallest size coins, dismissing them as "pennies." I occasionally interjected an encouraging comment, resisting the impulse to offer an adult solution. Even if it meant no solution would be reached, I wanted the children to work this out. Finally, after almost twenty minutes of pleading, threatening, demanding, and haggling, everyone agreed they were satisfied. While some inequalities between individual coin collections persisted, the fatigued players agreed to call the distribution fair. I was sympathetic, noting, "Sometimes it is hard work to make things fair."

While potentially useful in expanding the children's moral frameworks, these first two exercises were simply that—exercises. I also wanted to bring the search for fairness into the children's daily lives. It was time to come home to Cambridge and confront issues such as Miss D.'s exemption from meeting times. I was concerned that raising such issues directly would produce strong feelings that could derail a reasoned discussion, so I continued to use South Africa as a context in which to explore fairness. Specifically, one meeting time

I announced the arrival of a letter from Nelson Mandela. While Janet was skeptical about the letter's authenticity, she and the other children agreed to play along as I read:

> Dear Preschoolers,
>
> As you know, here in South Africa we have gotten rid of all our bad laws. Now we are trying to make things fair for everyone. One area where you could help us is day care, and making things fair for children. One problem is with sharing. Sometimes children bring in cards and presents for some of their friends, but not for everyone. Sometimes at the end of the day parents bring in food that their children then share with some classmates, but not everyone. At one day care center there is a child who gets to help set up snack, but no one else does. What should we do about these things to help make it fair? Thank you for your help.
>
> Sincerely,
>
> Nelson Mandela

The children got right to work. They brainstormed ideas that solved these South African problems that mirrored issues in our own classroom. Immediately, the idea of taking turns was forwarded—taking turns helping set up snack, and taking turns bringing in snack for everyone to share. James summed up the group consensus that "the teacher would say every day which day you bring in food and then every child would bring in food." Equity, with an adult as guarantor, was the ticket to fairness.

Then Joy interjected an interesting point into the conversation. Regarding the question of snacks she asked, "What if it's made out of sugar?" Michael was diabetic, and she was worried about her friend. Her concern provided a point of departure for me to challenge the children's thinking equating equity and fairness. I asked, "Does it have to be the same to be fair?" The children's overwhelming response was affirmative. I probed, pointing out, "Katie can't have wheat crackers. Should we only have rice cakes to make it fair for Katie?" Again, the response was a chorus of "Yes." But knowing several children's aversion to rice cakes, I was skeptical, so I asked incredulously, "So should we just have rice cakes in the preschool room?"

To some, this went too far, even in the search for fairness. Maddy cried out.

*Maddy:* It's not fair.

*Ben:* But you just said everything has to be the same. If you got to eat some wheat crackers or some chocolate, which Katie can't eat, then it wouldn't be the same and then it wouldn't be fair. Right?

*Michael:* Katie doesn't care.

*Ben:* What if she did care?

*Janet:* They could make a half for Katie and a half for the other kids.

*Ben:* But that would mean kids wouldn't get the same snack.

Janet thought for a minute, and then invoked the fact that the group ate snack at two separate tables.

*Janet:* Katie could eat rice cakes and so half could be rice cakes, and for the other table could be something else.

*Ben:* Janet, you're saying that giving everyone what they need is being fair even though its not the same. That's a different idea.

Here was my opening to talk about snack setup and Miss D. I began, "so if being fair means everyone gets what they need, what about snack setup? Denaea needs to help with snack to have a good day. So isn't that fair?" Maddy and Michael were hostile to this reasoning. Interestingly, Joseph had a kinder stance.

*Joseph:* I think it's fair.

*Ben:* Why?

*Joseph:* Because I love her.

Janet then offered a compromise, suggesting that two children could help set up snack, allowing Miss D. and the other children to simultaneously have turns. Maddy wasn't appeased, declaring, "It's not fair. Then none of the kids would be happy and they would make a face."

I couldn't resist one last challenge to Maddy and Michael, not because their position on the issue didn't have merit, but because they were so uncompromising in their stance that fairness demanded strict equality.

*Ben:* I have a question for Maddy and Michael. You are saying it has to be the same to be fair. But your families have two cars each. Joy's family only has one car and Denaea's family doesn't have any cars. Is that fair?

*Michael:* It feels fair to me.

*Ben:* Why is it fair if you get extra stuff, but it's not fair if someone else gets extra stuff?

*Michael:* It makes me mad.

*Ben:* I understand that it makes you mad, but is that fair?

*Michael:* I just want my best friends to have it.

*Ben:* I understand what you're saying, and it's hard. But sometimes you won't get exactly what you want and it will make you mad.

*Michael:* And then we'll have to work it out.

This was a fascinating discussion; one without a definite right answer. I reiterated the point that trying to make things fair is hard work. I then concluded that I would send our ideas to President Mandela, and that we would talk about this again.

There was one further point about fairness I was compelled to address, the children's incessant complaints about fairness over petty issues. While I knew the issues weren't petty to the children, there were times when I thought one more, "It's not fair" comment would drive me crazy. To indulge myself in a conversation on this issue, a few days later we received a second letter from Nelson Mandela. In it he thanked us for our ideas about fairness in South Africa, sympathized about how difficult it was to make things fair, and then offered a suggestion to help with our constant, contentious complaints about fairness. He wrote:

> First, make a list of all the things at your day care that aren't fair. Then, put each problem into one of three piles. The first pile is for problems that aren't fair and can be changed. The second pile is for problems that aren't fair and can't be changed. The third pile is for problems that aren't fair but it doesn't matter.

The children took President Mandela's suggestion very seriously. We dutifully made a list, and then classified each problem. While this did not end the children's clamoring for fairness, it did provide a vocabulary for addressing the issue. Over the next months I responded many a time, "Is this one of those not fairs that doesn't really matter?"

Clearly, our study of South Africa did not create twelve little angels who acted fairly in every situation. What I hoped it did do, by engaging the children in a topic filled with moral issues, was expand their thinking, furthering the somewhat inexplicable process of moral development.

## Nelson and James

The struggle for freedom in South Africa struck a chord deep in James' soul. In particular, he was captivated by the story of Nelson Mandela. He retold it to his parents in great detail, and was especially enthusiastic about Mandela's release from prison. James was so impressed that the preschoolers had received a letter from President Mandela that he continued the correspondence at home.

James' letter was to the point. With his mother providing assistance in spelling, James wrote:

Dear Nelson Mandela,

Thank you for your ideas.

Love,

James

I learned of James' letter when his mother asked me where she might send a message to the South African president. Not having to rely on the post for my previous letters, I did not have an address, but suggested sending the note to the South African embassy in Washington, D.C. Much to his parents' and my surprise, James soon received a reply from the capital. Written on the official letterhead of the Republic of South Africa, it read:

Dear James,

Thank you so much for the letter you have written to President Nelson Mandela. I am going to send it to him and I am quite sure he would be delighted to receive it. I, like you, am a great admirer of President Mandela (we call him Madiba in South Africa which means "Father" and "Headman" in Xhoa, the mother tongue of President Mandela).

I am very impressed that a young man of only four years of age can write a letter like yours. I will not be surprised to read, somewhere in the future, a best selling book by James Curtis.

With kind regard,

Yours sincerely,

Franklin A. Sonn

AMBASSADOR

James was exceedingly pleased to learn that his letter was being forwarded to Nelson Mandela.

The study of South Africa gave James a new hero. I am sure many readers applaud his choice, agreeing with my depiction of Nelson Mandela and the antiapartheid movement as heroic. My guess is, some may be critical. The critique that Nelson Mandela is not beyond reproach and that I presented a simplified version of history is true. Like other great leaders of the twentieth century, Mahatma Ghandi, Eleanor Roosevelt, and Martin Luther King, Nelson Mandela is human, with flaws both personal and political. Nelson Mandela is also certainly a hero, just as the apartheid system was categorically, undeniably wrong. Against great odds and involving much risk and personal sacrifice, Mandela led the struggle against apartheid with determination and dignity.

Children need heroes, and seek them out. Often the ones provided them are athletes or comic-book "superheroes." Heroic in terms of their power and achievements, these figures do not necessarily have any moral value. In light of the alternatives, I was especially pleased Nelson Mandela had become James' hero. It was a very worthy choice.

One afternoon during outside play, a month after the conclusion of our study of South Africa, Michele raced into the classroom. James was hot on her trail. "Remember when we studied South Africa," he called after her. "And when you couldn't vote. Well, it's the same thing." Curious to find out what the commotion was about, I questioned James. He explained that outside Michele had said only children with white skin could play in her game. "But that's not fair," he pointedly told me. "Remember South Africa?"

## Resources

To help children travel to South Africa, figuratively speaking, teachers need information and inspiration. For information, I recommend books. The most readable history of South Africa I've encountered is Leonard Thompson's *A History of South Africa* (New Haven: Yale University Press, 1995). Thompson covers the subject from soup to nuts, from precolonial times to the post-apartheid era. An excellent way to learn about the antiapartheid movement and Nelson Mandela is to do so firsthand. Mandela's autobiography, *Long Walk to Freedom* (Boston: Little, Brown, 1991) is a lengthy but very readable tale of hope and determination. Little, Brown has also put out an illustrated edition with an abridged text.

For inspiration, I suggest the cinema. The 1980s saw a series of powerful films set in apartheid South Africa. Richard Attenborough's *Cry Freedom* is the true story of the friendship that developed between Black activist Steven Biko and White journalist Donald Woods. Strong performances by Denzel Washington and Kevin Kline capture a relationship tragically cut short by Biko's murder in police custody. *A World Apart*, starring Barbara Hersey, is another true story, this about Ruth First and her family. First and her husband, Joe Slovo, were prominent among the progressive White South Africans who worked against apartheid. The film tells of some of their work, and of the wrenching impact being in opposition to the government had on their children. *A Dry White Season* is a fictionalized account of apartheid-era South Africa. Donald Sutherland plays a well-respected teacher and former sports star who is somehow clueless about the horrors of apartheid. When his gardener's son is killed in a demonstration in Soweto, Sutherland begins a journey that leads him to discover the injustices existing in his country.

Once the journey is under way, picture books set in South Africa are a tremendous teaching resource. Citations for the books mentioned above are:

Aardema, V. 1994. *Misoso: Once upon a Time Tales from Africa.* New York: Knopf.

Mennen, I., and N. Daly. 1992. *Somewhere in Africa.* New York: Dutton.

Stock, C. 1990. *Armein's Fishing Trip.* New York: Morrow.

Stock, C. 1993. *Where Are You Going Manyoni?* New York: Morrow.

In addition to these texts, I recommend:

*Ntombi's Song* by Jenny Seed with pictures by Anno Berry (Boston: Beacon Press, 1987). Set in rural South Africa, Ntombi is a young girl who has never ventured far from home. Sent to the store for the first time by herself, she confronts her fears of going through the forest by singing the song her family composed for her as an infant. Joy was very interested in this story, and adopted Ntombi's song as her own, marching around the classroom singing it. The idea of a personal song intrigues preschoolers, and writing such tunes is a nice spin-off project.

*Charlie's House* written by Reviva Schermbrucker and illustrated by Niki Daly (New York: Viking, 1989). Charlie Mogotsi is a young boy who lives with his mother and grandmother in a tin shack with a leaky roof. He dreams of a house with a TV and a room of his own. Acting on his dream, he builds a model of that house out of discarded materials found around his shanty town. The book is a good starting point for a discussion of the economic inequalities of apartheid-era South Africa. My students enjoyed constructing their own model houses out of recyclable materials.

*Not So Fast Songololo* by Niki Daly (Cape Town: Human and Rousseau, 1985). The story of a boy named Shepard and his gogo (grandmother) who travel together into the city on a shopping expedition. On the trip, Shepard, nicknamed Songololo, experiences the sights and sounds of a South African city. At the end of the trip Songololo is surprised by his grandmother, who spends some precious rands on a new pair of shoes for her grandson. This was a favorite story in my room, and the children loved rolling the name Songololo off their tongues.

*At the Crossroads* by Rachel Isadora (New York: Greenwillow, 1991). Isadora tells the story of a group of children waiting at the crossroads of their village for their fathers to come home from the mines. After an all-night wait, the children are finally rewarded with their fathers' return.

*The Day Gogo Went to Vote: South Africa, April 1994* by Elinor Sisulu (Boston: Little, Brown, 1996). Told from a young girl's perspective, this book tells of the girl's great-grandmother's efforts to participate in the first free election in South Africa. Truth be told, I enjoyed the book more than my students did, a full appreciation requiring a more mature perspective than preschoolers have. Still, the children related to the story on some level, especially after participating in the voting exercises described above.

I also recommend a couple South African folk tales. *Jackal's Flying Lessons,* written by Verna Aardema and illustrated by Dale Gotlieb (New York: Knopf, 1995), begins, "It was springtime in South Africa." It proceeds to tell the story of how jackal tricked mother dove into surrendering her babies and how, in turn, jackal was tricked by crane into returning (actually regurgitating) the fledglings. Enacting the story was a popular activity.

*Abiyoyo,* written by Pete Seeger and illustrated by Michael Hayes (New York: Macmillan, 1986), is the most famous South African folk tale among the preschool set. The story of a father and son who are ostracized from their village, then welcomed back as heroes after saving the town from a very unpleasant-looking giant, *Abiyoyo* has inspired generations of children out in the play yard.

I am a novice on the subject of South African music. What I can do here is report what I've heard and enjoyed, adding the disclaimer that there is a vast wealth of material available for exploration. Miriam Makeba is the grande dame of South African popular music. With a beautiful voice she delivers both soulful ballads and upbeat dance tunes. Two albums that span part of her career are *Live From Paris and Connkry* (Sonodisc, 1970), and *Eyes on Tomorrow* (Polygram, 1991).

For music specifically for children, Ladysmith Black Mambozo's *Gift of the Tortoise: A Musical Journey Through Southern Africa* is an enjoyable disk featuring stories and songs. Included is the tune "Aweemawa: The Lion Sleeps Tonight." The CD is put out by Music for Little People in Redway, California.

My favorite South African group is Juluka. A union of two guitarists, Johnny Clegg and Sipho Mchunu, Juluka plays upbeat songs that virtually force you to dance. Formed in the 1970s, the group was the first successful integrated band in South Africa. At least two Juluka CDs are available in the United States, *Scatterlings,* a 1996 rerelease (Rhythm Safari, Los Angeles), and *A Johnny Clegg and Juluka Collection,* put out by Putumayo World Music (627 Broadway, New York, NY 10012). Bandmember Clegg explains the group's music as a synthesis of Western-based rhythm structures and melodies mixed with Zulu lyrics and social commentary, seeking to "find meeting points between modern and traditional society, rural and urban experiences, exploring the many facets of the cultural reality of South Africa."

I want to thank two parents who visited South Africa, Gypsy Gallardo and Liz Gardner, for generously sharing their beadwork, fabrics, rands, and firsthand knowledge. Their enthusiasm for this wonderful country was contagious. I also want to thank my wife, Liz Merrill, for introducing me to the possibilities of epic travelogs. Her stories, which inspired my Ashraf tale, have made many a long family car ride more bearable, enchanting our sons with visions of adventures in far-off lands. Finally, University of Virginia professor Jennings Wagoner Jr. generously provided me some of his writings on Thomas Jefferson and education. I like to think the spirit of Jefferson's thinking about the importance of moral education in a democracy resides within this essay.

# 6

## And We Told Wonderful Stories Also: Storytelling

### Lindsay's Wonderful Idea

One of the most memorable moments of my teaching career occurred several years ago during a storytelling time. It was Lindsay's turn to tell a story to the class, and as she did so she had a truly wonderful idea. On the face of it, Lindsay was an unlikely candidate to have a wonderful idea while telling a story. A child with Down's syndrome, Lindsay's cognitive abilities lagged well behind the rest of the group's. Her speech consisted of one- and two-word utterances, limiting her ability to contribute at group times or participate in dramatic play. Throughout the year it had been a challenge to integrate Lindsay into classroom activities.

Still, Lindsay wanted to tell stories just like the other children. So on this particular day she was sitting in the storyteller's chair holding two pig puppets. The "tale" was unfolding in much the same way as her previous performances. To begin, the puppets said "hi" and "bye" to each other about a dozen times. Then the pigs pantomimed eating as Lindsay made chewing noises. Then the pigs went to sleep. At this point the effort could hardly be described as a compelling narrative.

Then something completely different occurred. Lindsay stood up, walked over to Jenny, the child immediately to her left, and had the pig puppets give her a kiss. The smile on Jenny's face inspired Lindsay to continue to Joey. Joey's positive response propelled Lindsay to Ashley. Ashley's laughter sent Lindsay on to Tony. And so on. After every classmate had received a kiss, Lindsay sat back down in the storyteller's chair, a huge smile on her face. The appreciative chorus of "thank you" coming from the audience confirmed to Lindsay that this was a wonderful idea.

Over the next few days, as other children took their turns telling stories, Lindsay's idea reappeared. Joey, David, and Nora all used the pig puppets in a similar fashion. Each time a storyteller circled the group bestowing kisses children would call out, "That's Lindsay's idea." The mention of her name brought back a smile to Lindsay's face.

It is impossible to say exactly what skills Lindsay learned during that story time, and certainly her achievement is not on any checklist of competencies that four-year-olds should master. Nevertheless, I attach great importance to her accomplishment. Lindsay's awareness that she had, that she could have, a significant idea was tremendously important to her learning and development. At that moment she had a place in the classroom *as a learner,* and she knew it. Recognizing the vital nature of what Lindsay did that day, I've adopted as my credo of education Eleanor Duckworth's (1987) belief that *the essence of pedagogy is to give learners the occasion to have wonderful ideas, and to let them feel good about themselves for having them.*

How does one provide the occasion for children to have wonderful ideas? I struggle with this fundamental question each day I'm in the classroom. Over the years I have begun to formulate some answers. This chapter contains some of these answers, describing how I try to provide the children in my class the occasion to have wonderful ideas about storytelling, and let them feel good about themselves for having them.

## Why Storytelling?

Five years before Lindsay had her wonderful idea, I was a novice teacher working at a Head Start program with my friend Anne Kornblatt. Anne and I alternated days leading meeting times, and to be honest, I dreaded my turn. Like many beginning teachers, I had difficulty managing large-group activities. During my meeting times most of the children were inattentive and some misbehaved. Trying to control these unruly students, I felt more like a police officer than an educator.

One morning before school, on my day to lead the meeting, Anne handed me a bright green "storytelling bag," which was to be one of the children's choices at exploration time. On a whim, I decided to use the bag at meeting. With the children gathered in a circle, I informed them I was going to tell a story, and opened the bag. Out tumbled a hole punch, a pencil, a crayon, a candle, and a stapler. Without a specific tale in mind, I began to ad lib. First, the crayon chased the pencil. Then the hole punch chased the crayon. Then the crayon and the pencil chased the hole punch. Hardly an inspiring story, but it didn't matter. The children were mesmerized, hanging on my every word. The meeting time was a pleasure. I was experiencing the power of storytelling.

Naturally, I pursued storytelling further, developing a repertoire of tales to tell my students. During these early years it was a one-way street; only I was telling stories at group times. Then I read *Wally's Stories* by Vivian Paley (1981), and learned of the possibilities of children telling stories. Inspired by Paley's writings, I made a place for the children to join me in storytelling.

How children tell stories in my classroom has evolved over the past ten years based on their reactions to the curriculum, and my propensity to experiment. The current incarnation of my storytelling program has three main features:

- adults telling stories
- children telling stories
- children preparing for their performances under my guidance

The storytelling program begins in September. At first, the daily story times involve only adult performances. More often than not, I'm the adult. My stories include international folk tales, original yarns often told with puppets, and reminiscences of childhood experiences. When they seem ready, generally by late October, I invite the children to take the storyteller's chair. The response to this invitation is always enthusiastic, so I assign each child a storytelling day. With a maximum of two daily performers the audience's attention span is generally not exceeded, and children get a turn telling every other week. On their storytelling day I meet with each child to help prepare for their performance. At these conferences I ask about the story's characters, setting, and plot. Children then rehearse while I listen appreciatively, ask clarifying questions, and make suggestions about the story's content and the teller's presentation style (e.g., face the audience; speak loudly).

The storytelling program runs for the entire year. In this way it is unlike other curricula described in this book, units that last at most a month. There are several reasons why we devote so much time to storytelling.

First, it is very useful for preschoolers to get up and talk in front of a group. For many adults, myself included, speaking in front of an audience is not an easy task. Presenting ideas in a coherent and interesting manner is not something that comes naturally. It involves gaining and coordinating a number of competencies—finesse with language, thinking on one's feet, an appreciation of humor and drama—all while having a sufficient comfort level to do this in front of other people. Despite the difficulties, orally presenting ideas is something children are called upon to do throughout their school careers. Practicing these skills in the intimate setting of preschool is a valuable experience, especially for shyer children. Reports from parents of former students confirm my sense that preschool experiences with storytelling help children overcome their natural reticence to speak in front of groups and offer a positive venue for children who are more outgoing and enjoy being the center of attention.

Second, telling stories helps prepare children for learning how to read and write. When I first began helping children tell stories I was unaware of the link between literacy and storytelling. A perusal of the scholarly literature (Snow 1983; Dickinson and McCabe 1991) alerted me to the important role storytelling plays in literacy development. When they begin school my charges will be taught to read by reading *stories*. In progressive classrooms, they will be taught to write by writing *stories*. I have been told by first-grade teachers that the children who have the hardest time with writing aren't those struggling with the mechanics of writing, but those who lack a sense of story.

A third, more theoretical but equally important reason is that storytelling gives children practice in what is called "decontextualized speech." Most young children's speech is about the here and now. Children tell us "I don't like *it*," "I want *that*" and "*he* hit me." Contextual cues—children pointing, adults surveying the environment, and shared experiences—support such discourse. So we understand that *it* is broccoli, *that* is a ball, and *he* is Dennis. The written word is a very different type of language. It is decontextualized, and with the exception of picture books, offers no nonwritten clues to help ascertain meaning. It is language about the then and there, taking us away in time and space. Storytelling is a step in the direction of decontextualized speech, often set out of the immediate context. However, oral stories aren't completely decontextualized. Tone of voice, gesture, and props help convey the meaning of the words. In this way storytelling serves as a bridge from the dominant language of early childhood to the more abstract language of literacy.

Storytelling has important implications for children in the future, but ultimately, I devote so much time to storytelling for a fourth, and more immediate reason: it is truly compelling curriculum. Year after year, the reactions of my students confirm this. Watching a child come forward to share a story is a wonderful sight. Often he or she has anticipated the event for several days, and is full of self-importance taking the storyteller chair. As the story begins, the teller scans the audience, searching for peer reactions. Do they become frightened during suspenseful scenes? Do they laugh at jokes? The audience, for their part, is listening intently. They attend as one would in a conversation, listening for responses to their own tales, or for events that deserve comment in future stories. The story completed, the teller returns to be part of the audience, often to be congratulated by friends. Details of the performance are the first things parents hear at pickup time.

The tremendous excitement about this activity stems from the centrality of storytelling to the human experience. The philosopher Daniel Dennett

(1991) observed, "Just as spiders weave webs and beavers build dams, people tell stories." Participating in this quintessential human experience makes the storytelling program compelling curriculum.

It has been almost fifteen years since Anne handed me that green bag, and I ventured into the realm of storytelling. Over the years nearly two hundred children have participated in my storytelling program. I have thought a great deal about how to create an environment where children can have wonderful ideas about storytelling. On this score I have much to say, from nitty-gritty suggestions about program management to four guiding principles for undertaking the endeavor. The remainder of this chapter expounds on these guiding principles:

1. Hearing stories, having role models, can support and encourage children's narrative endeavors.
2. Adult guidance, editorial assistance, can strengthen children's emerging storytelling skills.
3. Adult guidance must be offered in a sensitive, supportive manner. In other words, take care when you mess with someone's story.
4. The classroom community, the group, is central to the success of a storytelling curriculum.

While not the alpha and omega of running a storytelling program, these ideas will hopefully prove useful to teachers trying to help their students tell better stories.

## Role Models

Anyone who has spent time in an early childhood classroom is familiar with the phenomenon of children playing teacher. The phenomenon often occurs during the choice times which follow teacher-led meetings. Rather than electing to build with blocks, or paint, or dress up as firefighters, a number of children will stay behind in the meeting area. One of these children will sit in the teacher's chair and lead another meeting: "reading" books to the group, calling on the other children with questions, and disciplining unruly peers. Children can be quite skilled as they lead these sessions, and it is clear that much has been learned from careful observation of teachers.

Something powerful is at work here as children play teacher. Their observations both motivate and provide material for their play. In my storytelling program I did not set out to harness this power, I just happened to be telling stories. Reflection led me to the realization that my stories are a central feature of the program. Adult role models add to children's desire to tell stories as well as providing ideas about how to tell stories.

Four-year-olds have a conservative streak in their nature. Change is regarded with suspicion. New classroom activities are often approached with skepticism. Thus each year our movement class has a small core of nonparticipants who have decided preschoolers don't dance. Often I have a few children who politely refuse to paint. There are always several children who demur from singing. Invite some four-year-olds to tell a story in front of a group, and you are likely to hear at least one firm "No, thanks."

In contrast, for the past five years my storytelling program has achieved 100 percent participation. By now I take it for granted that everyone will tell stories, even those who won't dance, paint, or sing. While this is partly because their peers are doing it, many children's initial desire to tell stories comes from their observations of my storytelling. They want to come forward, sit in the storyteller's chair, and use my puppets. Having a role model gets them going.

Role models also supply children with information about how to tell stories. On a superficial level, this is apparent in the characters children use in their narratives. For several years, I had noticed the characters appearing in the children's stories often originated in my tales. One year I formally kept track of this phenomenon. Nearly two-thirds of the characters the children used came from my stories. Most popular were my puppets, who always retained their identities when the children used them. The children's stories were also populated with generic characters (e.g., a fox), along with characters who came from stories told by parents. Only 3 percent of the children's characters had commercial origins (e.g., Power Rangers), a heartening finding for teachers trying to direct children's imaginations away from the wasteland of Saturday morning cartoons.

On a deeper level, children also develop their sense of story by listening to stories. They learn how to organize their narratives, to use ritualized beginnings and endings, to sequence events, and provide necessary orientative information, in part, from role models. A spectacular example of how children use what they hear to fashion their own stories comes from four-and-a-half-year-old Beth.

Beth was an outgoing child with many friends and a wonderful sense of humor. She was one of the children who liberally borrowed from my stock of characters. Particular favorites of hers were my two pig puppets: Pig Pig and Perfect. In almost all of Beth's stories the pigs appeared, often in central roles. Sometimes they would be victims, fleeing terrible monsters. Other times they would be bad guys, perpetuating reprehensible acts. The pigs were vessels for expressing the range of Beth's emotions.

Over the year Beth heard me tell and retell Haitian folk tales about the lovable but bumbling farmer Uncle Booky. Several days after I told one such tale, Beth told a story starring the two pig puppets. In order to see how Beth used my model to help organize her story, I have taken the relevant sections of each story and displayed them in segments.

In my story, Uncle Booky walks from his farm to market. Arriving at the market:

1. Uncle Booky saw an old man eating a sandwich. He took a bite of the sandwich and Uncle Booky could tell that it tasted really good.

2. Uncle Booky went up to the man.

3. He said, "Excuse me sir, but what kind of sandwich are you eating?"

4. The old man didn't say anything because he was deaf and couldn't hear Uncle Booky's question.

5. So Uncle Booky repeated his question a little louder. "Excuse me, can you tell me what kind of sandwich you're eating?"

6. The man didn't hear and kept on eating his sandwich. Uncle Booky could tell that it was a very tasty sandwich.

7. Uncle Booky said, "Excuse me sir, but could you please tell me what kind of sandwich you are eating?"

In the folk tale, the old man continues to ignore Uncle Booky, bites into a red hot pepper, and screams, "We ah." Uncle Booky thanks the old man for the information about We Ah sandwiches, and embarks on a weeklong quest across Haiti in search of some We Ah.

According to her mother, Beth planned out her story at the family breakfast table the day of her performance. The story began with Pig Pig and Perfect going to a puppet show with their friends Joe Pizza and Machiko. At the conclusion of the show:

1. Pig Pig noticed something. It was a man walking down the street with something.

2. So he stepped out.

3. He said, "What are you carrying sir?!"

4. The man didn't tell him because he could not hear Pig Pig because he was too busy concentrating on walking.

5. So he said again, "Could you please. What are you carrying? What are you carrying?" he called.

6. But he [the man] still didn't answer.

7. So he [Pig Pig] said, "Could you please tell me what you are carrying?"

Beth's story went on to explain that the man didn't answer "because he had to concentrate on doing." Eventually though, the pigs went over to the man's house, riding on a giraffe. The story concluded in the Preschool Room where Pig Pig disrupted a meeting time by singing the ABCs (much to the teacher's consternation).

Even considering its source, the segment of Beth's story where Pig Pig questions the man to no avail is a remarkable piece of preschool storytelling. The facile use of language, the clear sequence of causally connected events, and the embedding of reported speech are all very impressive. It is a wonderful idea. This wonderful idea clearly owes a debt to the Uncle Booky tale. The similarities between the underlying structure of the two segments is impressive. Both passages begin with the main characters asking a question of a second character. The second characters do not respond, indeed are unable to respond, because they cannot hear the questions. The main characters then restate their questions to which, again, there are no responses. The wonderfulness of Beth's passage is not that she was able to copy this structure, but that she was able to use the organizational strategy in fashioning her own, very entertaining tale.

It is argued that adults should not present their work to children, particularly where the expressive arts are concerned. The fear is that role models will stifle children's creativity, that children will feel compelled to rigidly follow mature examples. This fear is not borne out in my experiences with the storytelling program. No child has ever exactly copied one of my stories. Their borrowing always involves transformation. Rather than a rigid model to follow, the adult stories are a resource that children are free to borrow from or to ignore. Role models provide the raw materials from which wonderful ideas can be fashioned.

## Editorial Assistance

Several years ago I was given a tour of a highly regarded day care center in the Boston area. The tour guide, the center's director, was justifiably proud of her organization and spoke at length about the quality of the staff. She commented on the teachers' dedication, their concern for the children, and about the engaging materials they presented the children to explore. "There's just one thing," the director added hesitantly, "The staff puts out great stuff for the children to interact with, but then they just observe. I wish they would interact more with the kids." "You mean you want them to teach more," I innocently responded. "Oh no!" the director said, recoiling from the word teach, "Just interact more."

My conversation with the director inadvertently hit upon one of the central issues of education: the role of adults in children's learning. At the heart of this issue are the questions: How much should students be directed and instructed? and To what degree should students be free to uncover and discover? The director's reaction points to a deep ambivalence many early childhood educators have toward teaching when it is interpreted as adult direction/guidance/interference in children's explorations of the world. I understand this ambivalence. There are good reasons to be wary of adult interference in children's learning. But equally true, adult guidance can support and stretch children's learning, making aspects of materials, competencies, and knowledge more accessible. There are times when providing skills will enhance, not stifle, creativity. This is certainly the case regarding storytelling.

What might adult guidance, editorial assistance in the present case, look like when helping preschoolers tell stories? For several years I tried to characterize and categorize the proper assistance teachers should provide. None of my nomenclatures proved satisfactory. I have given up the quest, realizing that what appropriate editorial assistance looks like changes for me each time I meet with a child to rehearse a story. What optimal guidance looks like resists formulaic definitions, depending as it does on the specifics of the individual child's storytelling proficiency and the state of the child-teacher relationship, as well as whatever else is going on in the classroom at the time of the conference.

While I've given up on a comprehensive delineation of editorial assistance, I still have many thoughts about how teachers can assist children in having wonderful ideas about storytelling. The best way for me to describe these thoughts is through an example. It is a long example, but consequently rich in explanatory power. The example is a child-teacher conference which occurred in May. It was approximately the fifteenth time Allister and I had rehearsed a story. Allister was a very friendly, easygoing child. He relished telling stories, and had asked several times that day if it was time to "chitchat" about his story yet. When the time came, this particular conversation lasted over ten minutes, a significant amount of one-on-one time in itself. What follows is a transcript of the conference. Commentary is inserted throughout to highlight issues involved when providing children with editorial assistance.

The conference took place in the book area. I invited Allister over to talk about his story. He began preparations immediately, bringing over two chairs to be "a house," a common prop among his cohort of storytellers. Wanting to know more about this particular house, I asked:

*Ben:* Where's this house going to be?

*Allister:* This one and this.

*Ben:* OK, so there are going to be two houses. Where are these two houses? Are they near the day care center?

*Allister:* No, this is a barn.

*Ben:* Oh, this is a barn. Is it a farm?

*Allister:* Yeah.

*Ben:* Oh, it's a farm. So are the animals sleeping in the house or the barn?

*Allister:* The barn.

*Ben:* In the barn. OK.

Allister then realized he needed some plastic farm animals, and ran off to the block area to collect them.

My editorial assistance had begun by focusing on the story's setting. This was a common starting point for these conferences, and Allister was very familiar with such questions. When Allister returned from the block area I shifted the discussion to the story's characters:

*Ben:* Does this farm have a farmer?

*Allister:* Umm . . . Umm . . .

*Ben:* Or just farm animals?

*Allister:* A farmer.

*Ben:* Who is the farmer?

*Allister:* Machiko [referring to a tiger puppet].

I asked about setting and characters because these are some of the main building blocks of stories. In directing Allister's attention to these facets I was alerting him to two important narrative elements. These were the type of questions I had asked Allister from the beginning of the year. My questioning then turned to a new area for us, the plot. For some children, such a line of inquiry would be inappropriate. Many preschoolers' stories are strings of unconnected events with no overarching organization. For children just learning about sequencing events, talk of plot is too advanced. Allister could sequence events, and I had recently begun asking him to consider what direction his stories might take. So I asked:

*Ben:* And in your story, are silly things going to happen? Are scary things going to happen?

*Allister:* Ummm. Silly.

*Ben:* So this is going to be a silly farm story?

*Allister:* Yeah!

*Ben:* Great. I'll listen for silly things and if I have any ideas for other silly things that might happen I'll mention them to you.

In retrospect, I should have been more open ended or offered more options (e.g., sad, happy, mysterious) about plot possibilities. Despite my error, Allister began rehearing his story, holding the tiger puppet.

*Allister:* Machiko was walking and he went down.

*Ben:* Ah-ha.

*Allister:* Went to the barn and he said, "Wake up animals. Wake up." Isn't that funny?

*Ben:* Yeah, I don't think the farmers usually say, "Wake up animals."

*Allister:* Yeah [laughs].

*Ben:* What did the animals do?

*Allister:* They didn't say anything and they go to eat.

*Ben:* OK.

*Allister:* Isn't that funny also?

*Ben:* A little funny. It would be funnier if they said something back to the farmer.

*Allister:* Yeah, animals can't talk.

*Ben:* That's right. So that would be funny.

I had just given Allister some very specific guidance. I am aware that this level of adult intervention makes many early childhood educators uneasy. It is important to point out my advice was not given as a directive, but as a suggestion. Educator Sylvia Feinberg calls such guidance, "Lightly dropped suggestions." Sylvia's favorite example of such adult assistance comes from the domain of painting. She describes a preschooler painting at the easel, creating a beautiful face. After the hair, mouth, and ears are in place it is time for the eyes. The child places a big gob of paint in the proper location, and it drips down the paper. The image ruined, the child X's out the entire face. A lightly dropped suggestion here would be to explain how wiping one's brush on the paint can eliminates excess paint, avoiding such mishaps. As with my suggestion about talking farm animals, the child can accept or reject the guidance, based on their inclination and readiness for such input. In this case, Allister took the talking animal suggestion and ran with it, coming up with a very funny idea.

*Allister:* Yeah. And the sheep say, "Go away farmer!" [Allister laughs]

*Ben:* That's funny.

*Allister:* And the pigs said. The pigs said, "Na na nee boo boo. You can't catch me. We are in the barn."

*Ben:* That's very silly.

*Allister:* Pig Pig goes up. Hop, hop, hop. Boink. Boink. Oops. Pig Pig fall down. Pig Pig and he climbed a tree. That's funny. Pigs can't climb trees.

After this comedic spurt Allister paused, and acted out a scene without any words. Focusing on physical humor, he had the plastic farm animals bumping into each other and falling down. These nonverbal stretches appeared in most of Allister's stories. While they delighted his four-year-old audience, they bored me. In this rehearsal, I wanted to focus Allister on the narrative. Slapstick was sure to appear in his performance.

As mentioned, Allister seemed ready to produce a story with a plot, moving in the direction of many five- and six-year-olds who begin to structure their stories around a narrative high point (McCabe 1991). We enjoyed a very positive relationship, so I felt comfortable pushing Allister some. To nudge him toward plot development I asked, "Are there going to be any scary parts of this story?" Initially resistant to the challenge, Allister replied with a curt, "No." When I asked, "Any problems that the farmer has to solve?" he took the bait, answering with a tentative, "Yes." I moved quickly to have him elaborate:

*Ben:* What's the problem? Is it a problem with the barn? With a storm or something?

*Allister:* The barn.

*Ben:* What's going to happen with the barn?

*Allister:* It's going to fall down.

*Ben:* Oh no! I'd like to hear that part.

*Allister:* Why?

This was a fascinating question, speaking to Allister's emerging sense of story. Our discussion had created a very teachable moment. Why would it be interesting for his audience to hear about a problem with the barn? I explained:

*Ben:* Because I think it sounds interesting. I'm wondering what the farmer is going to do when the barn falls down and how you are going to tell about it. I think the kids will be really interested in this too.

Allister had to think about this, and I had to let him think. Any further input would have crossed the line, taking the initiative away from Allister, and making the narrative mine rather than his. Allister sat quietly, considering the situation. After what was a very long minute for me (worrying that I had indeed pushed too far) he knocked over the chair representing the barn and explained, "And the barn fall down." "Crash!" I called out, relieved at Allister's breakthrough. He continued:

*Allister:* Crash it goes. And the barn fall down and the parrot and Machiko and all the farm animals went running, running, running, running to see what is going on. And it has fire in it. And Machiko quickly, quickly find a phone and called. Called the fireman. And the fireman drive to the barn. And he said, "Look, our barn is on fire." And all the animals came. And they all looked.

After this narrative burst Allister paused. He seemed unsure where to go next. To help him continue, I asked for some evaluation of the events.

*Ben:* How did they feel? Were they sad or scared?

*Allister:* They are sad.

*Ben:* 'Cause their house is burning down. Yeah.

*Allister:* And the fireman quickly put the water on it and, and it looked better. But they don't know how to put it up again.

*Ben:* To put the barn back up?

*Allister:* Yeah.

Allister paused again. By now he had told a long, complex story for a preschooler. To guide him to a conclusion, I suggested, "Machiko is a farmer. Do you think she knows how to put the barn back up?" Allister replied, "Yep. But it is too big for her. It's too big for her so she has to climb a mountain."

"Why does she have to climb a mountain?" Watching Allister raise the tiger puppet over his head, I was able to answer my own question.

*Ben:* Oh, so she'll be taller.

*Allister:* Yeah.

*Ben:* Oh, OK, and the mountain is your head. I get that. And then what does she do when she is at the top?

*Allister:* Jump on the barn and back up!

*Ben:* Great, that was great.

To my mind, the story had reached a natural conclusion, but, to my surprise, Allister continued telling. He described how some baby pigs nursed from their mother (his mother had recently given birth to a baby boy), and how all the animals went to sleep. He then announced, "I'm done."

Before Allister went off I wanted to recap what we had discussed, making explicit some of the key points covered:

*Ben:* That was a fun story. I liked the beginning. It was very funny.

*Allister:* Why?

*Ben:* Because there were all those silly things. And I really enjoyed listening to the problem about the barn falling down and being on fire and how Machiko solved it.

*Allister:* Yeah. Maybe when I tell that part in my story they will be scared.

*Ben:* Yeah. They might be scared.

Many teachers, on hearing about this preparatory conference, want to know what the story performance was like. A half-hour later Allister was in the storyteller's chair. As his classmates watched, he carefully placed some plastic animals in "the barn." He then turned to me and pleaded, "I forgot the story, Ben."

I was not surprised nor disheartened by Allister's memory lapse. Children often look like they are losing ground when they are taking risks and trying something new. Allister's plea actually was the result of a developmental leap in his storytelling abilities. This was Allister's most complex and planned-out story. In his mind, stories were no long random happenings where performances and rehearsals bore little resemblance. There was now a correct way of telling his tale. As often happens when children gain a greater sense of the permanency of their stories, he was requesting assistance because he wanted to get it right.

After I reminded Allister about Machiko and her humorous conversation with the animals, he was off. The performance resembled the rehearsal in its general plotline, though in an abridged fashion. Allister told about the animals talking back to the farmer. He then warned the group that something "very scary" was about to happen. When the audience gasped, Allister reassured them not to be frightened, and went on to tell of the barn's destruction and reconstruction.

Unlike the rehearsal, I asked few questions and offered little guidance during Allister's performance. As a result, the quality of his narrative suffered, but this was beside the point both for Allister and myself. For Allister, the point of the performance was to connect with his audience. The way to do that was to tell something silly to get a laugh, or tell something scary to get a gasp of fright. A compelling story line, though useful, was not essential in making this social connection.

I too, understood the performance in social terms. In my mind, our work improving narrative skills had been accomplished. Some day Allister would be able to do independently what he did with my assistance during the conference. That assistance was helping Allister build a sense of story. My questions about setting, characters, and plot provided an implicit structure which Allister would eventually internalize. His future stories would be an implicit dialogue, answering questions about where the story was taking place, who was in the story, and what problems arose and were solved.

That would be in the future. At this point Allister needed assistance to tell stories with a plot and humor, and my guidance helped Allister take his storytelling to a new level. I find his idea of the pigs saying "na na nee boo boo" very funny, and the drama of the barn fire compelling. Allister was very proud of these ideas, and I think they are wonderful. That his ideas were the fruits of collaboration does not, in my mind, make them any less wonderful.

## Take Care When You Mess with Someone's Story

Allister's conference involved a calculated risk. It is a risk inherent in any interaction between two people with unequal power and knowledge. The risk was that my intervention could have taken away Allister's initiative, making the story more mine than his. Doing so would have diminished Allister's interest in storytelling, and damaged his confidence as a learner.

I am well aware of the danger of teacher interference in learning from personal experience, vividly recalling a high school English teacher named Ms. Borman. It seemed that whatever I did in Ms. Borman's class was wrong. No matter how hard I tried, my corrected papers drowned in a sea of red ink. All of Ms. Borman's verbal critiques were corrections of my works' shortcomings. I remember, after submitting several unappreciated drafts of a final project, I felt like screaming, "If you know so much why don't you write the damn paper yourself!" I may have learned some about the mechanics of English from Ms. Borman, but the lesson I retained from her class was that I didn't like writing. It took almost twenty years to unlearn that lesson.

You don't have to be a Ms. Borman to derail children's storytelling efforts. The editorial assistance of caring, supportive teachers can unintentionally subvert beginning storytellers. Facing the very difficult task of constructing a narrative, children will voluntarily abdicate control to more experienced tellers. Complicating the task is the fact that how stories are organized, their structure, is a cultural phenomenon, and that teacher input can run counter to ways of narrating children are learning at home. Providing editorial assistance is a delicate business, and even well-intentioned efforts can inflict harm. I urge great caution when you involve yourself with a child's story.

Support for my plea comes from the experience of Caleb in the storytelling program. A classmate of Allister's, Caleb was a quiet child, more comfortable expressing himself in drawings than in words. He had several good friends at day care, but preferred playing with them one at a time. This play was very action-oriented, involving superheroes, dinosaurs, and saber-toothed tigers. While it was clear Caleb liked me, he did not always seem at ease in my presence. His regard for me as an authority figure was in contrast to the casual relationships I had with most of his compatriots. This formal way of relating to adults was instilled by his mother, a forthright, energetic, loving Nigerian American woman who, by the prevailing norms of the day care center, was strict with her son.

From the onset, Caleb was an enthusiastic participant in the storytelling program. He once even gave up a trip to an amusement park with his father in order to stay at day care to tell his story. I spent the beginning of the program getting to know Caleb as a storyteller. His initial narratives were action-packed dramas told with puppets. They had some sense of sequencing, and hinted at a plot. The second story Caleb told during the year is a good example of these early tales. The story, entitled "The Earth of Anna," began with an alligator puppet named Anna going to visit an abrasive but kindhearted monster named Bubla:

Anna was sleeping. And she ate some fresh pizza. And watched TV. And she went down there where Bubla's cousin and Bubla was. And she was going to go. She dressed all up. And he walked. And he ran. And he opened the door. He [Anna] said "hi." He [Bubla] said "come in." And he came in. And he came out and talked to Anna in the house. They talked so many. They went around here. "I guess you got to go now." And he [Bubla] pushed him [Anna] out of the house. They were sleeping again.

Bubla went on the boat ship. And saw Captain Rebecca. And she smelled steam. And they turned into pirates. And there were a lot of pirates. He [Bubla] was going to get on some gold. The pirate boat was coming close to that very boat. It was coming closer. And he jumped in Anna's boat. And he took him on his boat. His bad boat. And tied him up. And he [Bubla] tied his [Anna's] hands up like this. And he was walking and walking. And she splashed in the water. He was drowning. But he had a secret that he was going to steal his boat. He stealed it.

And there was foxes. Bad foxes. Anna's foxes came. And they runned back on their boat and paddled. Fast. But one of the pirates splashed in the water. And there was one pirate left. But the wolf was trying to beat up Bubla. And he was fighting. He was trying to kick the wolf. But it wanted to swim. He put on his bathing suit.

And the S.S. Mary Poppins came with the preschoolers to help Anna the Alligator. And he splashed in the water quickly. He went on the preschoolers boat. And they came back on. Just Bubla.

And then he turned into a pirate. Bubla and his cousin. And they're turning. Bubla turned into. Back to Bubla. A good Bubla. And this one said, "Oh, I want to go on a boat." He went on. And he saw some pirates coming closely. And the end.

The story, like its title, is both intriguing and confusing. The intrigue comes from moments of high drama, such as the appearance of the *S.S. Mary Poppins,* hinting at possibilities for exciting plot developments. The confusion comes from a misuse of pronouns (e.g., Anna starts off as a she, but soon changes into a he), a tendency for the narrative to ramble, and a failure to explain the meaning of "the earth of Anna." What is most striking about the story is its nonstop action. The characters are in constant motion, eating, dressing, walking, talking, running, fighting, and going. Even the conclusion is presented as another event, "*And* the end."

After listening to a half a dozen of Caleb's stories, I thought I had a general sense of his narrative development, and where I might provide editorial assistance to stretch his abilities. I wanted him to be more explicit when describing the action in his stories, and hoped to move him toward a more developed plot. I had a clear agenda for Caleb, an agenda I felt would help further his literacy development.

During our conferences over the next few months, I continually asked Caleb clarifying questions about his action-packed dramas. I also wondered out loud if there were going to be any problems or scary parts in his stories. At first, Caleb dutifully answered these inquiries. But then he began to withdraw, pleading ignorance about the events in his own narrative. Our first conference in March is an example. As Caleb quietly played with a pig puppet, I asked:

*Ben:* What's she doing? I see she's crossing her arms, but what's it all about?

*Caleb:* She's doing it this way.

*Ben:* Ah-ha. Why is she doing that?

*Caleb:* I don't know.

*Ben:* You don't know. OK. And she just twisted around?

*Caleb:* Yes.

*Ben:* Why?

*Caleb:* I don't know.

These "I don't knows" were becoming increasingly common during our story conferences. In retrospect, they were signals that my editorial assistance was not connecting with Caleb.

The failure of my editorial assistance was also apparent in the stories Caleb was telling. Despite the theory, which held out the promise that my questioning would be internalized, there were no discernable improvements in Caleb's stories. To my mind, the quality of his narratives was deteriorating. Caleb was explaining less, focusing more and more on the physical actions of the puppets. Minutes could go by with the only vocalizations being the sound effects accompanying puppets crashing into each other.

Four months after his first performance Caleb told an untitled tale using Bubla, a pig puppet, and three frog puppets (one named Joe Pizza). It was a struggle for me to get much story out of Caleb. Only through my insistence that he "tell with words" what was being acted out did the following narrative emerge:

> Hop. He's [a frog] jumping. She trying to find the log. Jump. Peep. Peep. Making little peeps. Then comes Joe Pizza. He's sleeping. And he turns into a tadpole. Then a frog. They sit together. Then comes Pig Pig. He's going to think and then he's going to ride on the frog. Bong. They went on top of each other. Then comes Bubla. You know what he's going to say? "Go away!" Then went the dinosaur. Walk. Bonk. "Throw out the canister." He said, "throw out the canister." He went in here. Then he came out. Then went this one [a third frog puppet]. Like that. Like this. Bong. Dem, dem. He's thinking. Bong. Hop. He went like this now. They are going to a park. Go down the slide. Shooo. Then came Joe Pizza. "Go away!" Boom. He said the

thing what Bubla said. Slide. Boom. He jumped. He's turning. He sits down. He broke off his tail. Look what he's doing. He wiped his nose one day. This is the scary part. Caught Pig Pig. Walking. Jumps. He's down in the tunnel. He's rolling. Shhhh. He went in the tunnel. Then the frog comes. Jump. He jumps. Where Pig Pig is. He helps Bubla get out. Jump, jump, jump, jump. They're jumping in the water. Jump. The end.

I had little appreciation for this story. Besides finding it dull, it seemed to lack any coherency. To my ear, the jumping, bonging, and talking were completely random. It seemed far from the kind of narrative that would enhance Caleb's literacy development. In retrospect, I realize I sold the story short. A closer look at the narrative reveals a clear structure.

To understand my reevaluation of Caleb's story, and the reason for my original low esteem for the narrative, the notion of cultural variations in storytelling style must be introduced. The next few pages provide a thumbnail sketch of this complex idea. Because it is an important idea for teachers to be familiar with, I encourage further reading on the subject (Dyson and Genishi 1994; Michaels 1991).

How children organize their stories, just as how they relate to adults, approach self-help skills, and view school, is a cultural phenomenon. Scholars of narrative have identified distinct cultural styles of storytelling (Cazden 1988; Gee 1991; Keebler 1995; Mistry 1993). For example, White, middle-class children often come to school telling tales with a linear, problem-resolution structure. In this way, their stories follow the organizational pattern of a typical Hollywood movie. Stories open by setting the scene (e.g., introducing Dorothy and Toto) and defining a problem (e.g., how to get back to Kansas). A generally sequential set of events leads to the resolution of the problem (e.g., the trip to the Emerald City ends in the eventual return to Kansas). The story concludes with a short coda (e.g., Dorothy talking about her experiences with Auntie Em).

"Flapper Turns Five," a story told by Sarah on her fifth birthday, is a lovely example of such a linear, problem-resolution narrative. The story begins with Sarah introducing the main character, and telling about his problem:

> One day there was a baby bat. Mom said, "Let's fly." The baby bat flapped his wings. He could not fly. So his mother called him Flapper. Every day she tried to teach him to fly, but she couldn't teach him.

We then hear about efforts to resolve the problem:

> Then the mom's baby went to school to teach the baby bats how to fly. But every time the teacher said, "Flap your wings" Flapper couldn't fly.

> When he turned five they went to the school. And she said, "Flap your wings." And then Flapper flapped his wings, and then he flew!

> Then he never wanted to go down where he lived. He had too much fun flying. Mom said, "You'll break your wings." And Flapper broke his wings. And then they never grew back again.

Fortunately for all, the problem is eventually resolved:

> When Flapper turned eleven Mom said "I think you are ready to go to a different school." Then the next day they went to a teenager school. That was his new school. The end.

Sarah makes wonderful use of her cultural pattern of storytelling to tell a tale rich in psychological meaning.

Many African American children come to school telling topic-associating tales. These narratives are organized around a common theme rather than a particular problem. Stories may skip around in setting and temporal sequence, but like a piece of jazz music, events are linked together by a common motif. A tale told by six-year-old Leona utilizes this organizational plan with wonderful effect (Gee 1991). (The story was collected by Sarah Michaels and Courtney Cazden.) Leona begins her tale by stating an overarching point, a point she will return to at the end of her story:

> It's Friday the 13th. And it's bad luck day. And my grandmother's birthday is on bad luck day.

Leona then proceeds to explore the first of three themes: the baking of cakes by various family members:

> And my mother's baking a cake. And I went up to my grandmother's house while my mother is baking a cake. And my mother was baking a cheesecake. My grandmother was baking whipped cream cupcakes. And we both went over to my mother's house. And then my grandmother had made a chocolate cake. And then we went over to my aunt's house. And she had made a cake. And everybody had made a cake for Nana. So we came out with six cakes.

A second theme, her grandmother's eating of cakes (or in the case of cheesecakes, not eating them) is then described:

> Last night my grandmother snuck out. And she ate all the cake. And we hadda make more. And we was sleeping. And she went in the room and gobbled 'em up. And we hadda bake a whole bunch more. She said "mmmmm." She had all chocolate on her face. Cream. Strawberries. And then all came out. And my grandmother had ate all of it. She said "what's this cheesecake doing here?" She didn't like cheesecakes. And she told everybody that she didn't

like cheesecakes. And we kept making cakes and she kept eating 'em. And we finally got tired of making cakes. And so we all ate 'em.

The third theme, her grandmother and the bakery, is then introduced:

And now today's my grandmother's birthday. And a lot of people making a cake again. But my grandmother is going to get her own cake at her bakery. And she's gonna come out with a cake that we didn't make 'cause she likes chocolate cream. And I went to the bakery with her. And my grandmother ate cupcakes. And she finally got sick on today. And she was growling like a dog 'cause she ate so many cakes.

The story then concludes where it began: "And I finally told her that it was Friday the 13th: bad luck day."

Leona's tale does not fit into a first-grade story map. A teacher looking for a narrative which tells about one important thing would have difficulty with the story. Still, it is a wonderful narrative, following a clear cultural pattern of storytelling.

Using the lens of cultural variations in storytelling style provides a way of understanding Caleb's untitled story, revealing a clear organizational plan. Caleb combines the two approaches to structuring narrative described above, one learned at home and the second learned at day care. In the first half of the tale Caleb is topic-associating, the topic being characters. Beginning after an initial "hop," he introduces one character after another in a somewhat parallel fashion:

*He's [a frog]* jumping. She trying to find the log. Jump. Peep. Peep. Making little peeps.

*Then comes Joe Pizza.* He's sleeping. And he turns into a tadpole. Then a frog. They sit together.

*Then comes Pig Pig.* He's going to think and then he's going to ride on the frog. Bong. They went on top of each other.

*Then comes Bubla.* You know what he's going to say? "Go away!"

*Then went the dinosaur.* Walk. Bonk. "Throw out the canister." He said, "throw out the canister." He went in here. Then he came out.

*Then went this one [a third frog puppet].* Like that. Like this. Bong. Dem, dem. He's thinking. Bong. Hop. He went like this now. They are going to a park. Go down the slide. Shooo.

*Then came Joe Pizza.* "Go away!" Boom. He said the thing what Bubla said. Slide. Boom. He jumped. He's turning. He sits down. He broke off his tail. Look what he's doing. He wiped his nose one day.

Introductions made, Caleb switches to a problem-resolution structure, stating:

> *This is the scary part.* Caught Pig Pig. Walking. Jumps. He's down in the tunnel. He's rolling. Shhhh. He went in the tunnel. Then the frog comes. Jump. He jumps. Where Pig Pig is. He helps Bubla get out. Jump, jump, jump, jump. They're jumping in the water. Jump. The end.

All said, this story does not shine the way Sarah's or Leona's does. This is, in part, due to the fact that much of the narrative meaning was being acted out by puppets and remained unspoken. However, there is certainly more organization here than I initially gave credit for.

Because I was not understanding Caleb's stories, and because of the possibility that my lack of appreciation was due to the fact that my ear wasn't tuned to his cultural style of storytelling, I should have trod lightly with my editorial assistance. Instead, I continued to press ahead with my agenda. The problem was, the harder I pushed, the more Caleb withdrew. A crisis had to arise before I fully understood that my editorial assistance was being counterproductive.

The crisis occurred in mid-May. It was a hot day and the children, not yet acclimatized to the summerlike weather, were restless. Caleb came forward to tell his story, but, using few words to describe the puppets' actions, quickly lost his audience. Impatient with the continuing lack of narrative progress, I broke my own rule not to interfere with children's performances, and asked several clarifying questions. I prodded Caleb to "use more words." Caleb responded with short answers, and then continued in his nonverbal mode. Some of the children, who had learned through role models how to provide editorial assistance, joined in the calls for "more words." This proved to be too much. Pierced by his peers' perceived heckling, Caleb became very upset. He left the storyteller's chair in tears, running off to a far corner of the room.

While insensitive to my impact on Caleb before this moment, I suddenly realized how he felt. He felt like I did in Ms. Borman's class, deflated, defeated, and stupid. I immediately went over and apologized. Thanks to our solid relationship, I was able to repair some of the damage. I offered him opportunity to tell another story the next day. He accepted, and perked up.

Caleb's flight from the storyteller's chair served as an important reminder to me about the risks inherent in trying to direct children's learning. It is a timely reminder in today's pedagogical climate. Recently I viewed a video entitled *Vygotsky's Developmental Theory* (Davidson Films 1994), which highlights some ideas of the Soviet psychologist Lev Vygotsky. Vygotsky's work, which is currently very popular in educational circles, has important messages for teachers, including the importance of adult guidance in children's learning. The video did a nice job explaining the implications of Vygotsky's theory, but there was one segment I found upsetting. It showed a teacher working on counting skills with a preschool boy. The teacher was trying to help the child develop the idea of a one-to-one correspondence between numbers counted and physical objects observed. To do so, the teacher had set up a row of twenty blocks. The boy was shaky on the task, tending to skip an occasional block while counting. As he counted from one to twenty, the teacher held the boy's finger, directing it toward each block to make sure none were missed. I reacted very negatively to the technique, thinking, "I'd want to slap anyone who did that to me." Later in the video it showed the same boy counting the blocks independently as proof that work in conjunction with adults advances mathematical development. Indeed, the boy now counted each of the twenty blocks. But he did so in a disturbing way. He didn't just count, he knocked over each block as he came to it, barking out the numbers. He seemed angry. He had been taught to count, like it or not. The problem was, he didn't seem to like it.

Learning is more than a cognitive activity; it is an emotional one as well. Learning is very personal. It can be very exciting, especially when pursing one's own thinking or feeling competent. It can also be very frustrating, especially when one feels incompetent or not in control. This is particularly true when it comes to narrative. Stories can be very personal. The stories people tell represent who they are; how they present themselves to the world. In some ways I was lucky that Caleb's frustration precipitated a crisis. He let me know I had to back away from my editorial assistance, restoring the delicate balance between adult guidance and child initiative. Signals from other children may be more subtle, which is why teachers must take care when messing with someone's story.

The lesson of Caleb's experience is not that teachers have no role in helping children tell stories. My work with Allister is a clear statement to the contrary. Rather, the lesson of Caleb's experiences is that providing editorial assistance must be individualized. How much to intervene, when to push, and when to let a child go on without direction depends on the student. As with all teaching, helping children tell stories is a process involving experimentation, reflection, and continual revision. Mistakes will happen, but unlike Ms. Borman, most teachers will make amends.

## It Is the Group

No matter how inspired my stories, no matter how skilled and sensitive my editorial assistance, the curriculum would never have taken off if the children weren't telling their stories to valued friends and teachers. We tell stories to communicate, and the opportunity to tell the group is what drove the program. Hints of the social nature of the program have appeared throughout this chapter. Now I want to make it explicit: it is the group.

The centrality of the group is illustrated by a storytelling time held one January afternoon. Three children were slated to tell stories: Maddy, Denaea, and James. This was an odd threesome. Maddy was the queen of the classroom and for good reason. Friendly, self-assured, and physically attractive, she was a good friend and a skillful player. She was fun to be around and the children gravitated toward her. Denaea was a social outcast. Volatile and antisocial, she had great difficulty connecting with other children. James was the new kid on the block, only a few weeks off the plane from England. He was very verbal and intellectually had much to offer as a playmate, but his social skills were uneven. His proclivity to hit sometimes left him ostracized from this tightly knit group.

I avoid scheduling three storytellers in a day, three performances being generally too long for a preschool audience. A snow day earlier in the week had forced this unusual situation. Fearing the crowded program would test the audience's attention span, I braced for a fair amount of group management. I was pleasantly surprised that intervention was not required to focus the group on the storytellers.

Maddy was the first to take the storyteller's chair. Holding two pig puppets, she began in a loud, clear voice:

> Pig Pig and Perfect woke up. They got dressed and went down stairs. Then they ate oatmeal. Then they went for a walk in the forest. Then there was a monster with six heads and ten thousands arms who put them in the dungeon.

The audience recoiled in horror at this terrifying news. "I'm scared," Janet cried out. Max and Jack held hands.

Fortunately for the pigs, the preschoolers were also out in the woods. Through cunning, teamwork, and sheer bravery, the children rescued the pigs. The story's conclusion found everyone safely back at day care. Janet, Max, and Jack breathed deep sighs of relief.

Returning to her seat, Maddy was showered with compliments. "I liked it when the monster came," Max began. "I liked your story because it was so scary," Michael continued. "I liked when we saved the pigs," Michele recalled. Maddy sat quietly, a twinkle in her eyes, basking in the praise.

Denaea followed Maddy to the storyteller's chair. She held the same two pig puppets and began a "Popcorn Party" story, the details taken from a narrative I had told the class numerous times:

Pig Pig and Perfect were alone at their house. They were hungry, so they decided to have a popcorn party. So they called up the preschoolers. Ring, ring. "Hello Maddy, want to come to the popcorn party?"

Maddy responded affirmatively, and Denaea continued around the circle to Michele and then to Max. Both accepted their invitations. So far, all was proceeding as expected. But when Denaea addressed Michael, the story took a delightfully unexpected turn:

*Denaea:* Hello Michael, can you come to the popcorn party?

*Michael:* Yes, Saturn.

*Denaea:* I'm not Saturn!

The audience exploded in laughter. Denaea smiled. The fun was just beginning. Next in line was Joseph:

*Denaea:* Hello Joseph, can you come to the popcorn party?

*Joseph:* Yes, Pluto.

*Denaea:* I'm not Pluto!

Tremendous laughter again. Denaea's invitations to Jack and Janet brought similar responses and hilarity. All the invitations issued, the group, following Denaea's lead, mimed eating popcorn. For good measure, Denaea passed out imaginary slices of pizza. The story ended with smiles on everyone's faces, and applause for the teller.

Up next, James sat with the two pig puppets and a subway map of Boston. He explained that the pigs and the preschoolers had decided to take a trip on the Green Line. An early reader, James used his map to explain:

They went to Lechmere and got on the train. Then they went to North Station. Then they went to Haymarket. Then the went to Government Center where the Blue Line comes in.

A twist then arose in this recitation of stations. When James explained, "Then they went to Park Street where the Red Line comes in," Jack asked, "Did they get off there?" James answered negatively. But at the next stop, Boylston, it was James who asked the audience, "Did they get off there?" "No," answered Jack, Max, and Maddy correctly. Arlington was the next stop. "Did they get off there?" James asked rhetorically. A more resounding "No" from the crowd. The next stop was Copley. "Did they get off there?" the audience was asked, and this time everyone was with the program, enthusiastically crying out "No!" This call-and-response continued to the end of the line, Riverside, where the weary travelers finally disembarked.

Leaving the storyteller's chair with a big smile, James approached Maddy and Denaea. He exclaimed, "We all told stories with Pig Pig and Perfect!" Bonded by the common characters in their stories, the three embraced. For Denaea and James in particular, this was a special moment. They were part of the group. The warm feelings extended beyond the threesome to the entire class, which seemed to realize the importance of the event.

That January afternoon was a dramatic example of what happens during story times because of the group. Looking over the three performances, it is fair to say each contained a good, if not wonderful, idea. These wonderful ideas emerged from the group nature of the activity. Denaea and James' stories were directly changed for the better through group interactions. The heroes of Maddy's story were the audience members. How the storytellers felt about their ideas had everything to do with the group. The bottom line is, none of the performers would have told these stories without the audience.

One of the things we do in my preschool room is tell stories. Everyone does it. It is part of who we are. The relationship of the storytelling program and the group is a two-way street. As that story time in January demonstrates, the program contributes to the group, building community by creating a warm sense of connectedness among the children in the class.

## And We Told Wonderful Stories Also

On her last day in the preschool Mollie, a classmate of Lindsay, sat with her friends for our final meeting. I asked the children what they liked best about the year. Their responses varied. Some recalled specific curriculum units. Some talked about field trips taken. One child mentioned the snack he had eaten that day. Then Mollie raised her hand, and added, "And we told wonderful stories also."

Mollie's feelings, while important, were not unique. Each year the storytelling program captures my students' imaginations. Each year I hear of children like Beth, who anticipate and prepare for their stories in advance. Each year there are children like Allister who can hardly wait for an opportunity to rehearse their stories. Each year there are children like Caleb who forego exciting activities with their families so they can tell their stories. Each year there are days like the one in January when Maddy, Denaea, and James performed. Each year there are children like Mollie who choose the storytelling program as the highlight of their preschool year.

The reason is clear. When the story time is going well there is a magical feel to it. It is a feel that the children share with each other and with me. It is a feel that I as a teacher cherish. It is the feel of children fully engaged in compelling curriculum.

## Resources

My storytelling program clearly owes a debt to the academic literature. Foremost among these is the work of Lev Vygotsky, who wrote so convincingly of the social nature of development. Other theorists and researchers have been drawn upon as well. Citations for the works referred to in this essay are:

Cazden, C. 1988. *Classroom Discourse: The Language of Teaching and Learning.* Portsmouth, NH: Heinemann.

Dennett, D. 1991. *Consciousness Explained.* Boston: Little, Brown.

Dickinson, D., and A. McCabe. 1991. "A Social Interactionist Account of Language and Literacy Development." In *The Language Continuum,* edited by J. Kavanaugh, 1–40. Parkton, MD: York Press.

McCabe, A. 1991. Preface: "Structure as a Way of Understanding." *Developing Narrative Structure,* edited by A. McCabe and C. Peterson, ix–xvii. Hillside, NJ: Erlbaum.

Paley, V. 1981. *Wally's Stories.* Cambridge, MA: Harvard University Press.

Snow, C. 1983. "Literacy and Language: Relationships During the Preschool Years." *Harvard Educational Review* 53: 165–89.

For those interested in reading more about cultural variations in storytelling styles, I recommend:

Dyson, A., and C. Genishi. 1994. *The Need for Story: Cultural Diversity in the Classroom and Community.* Urbana, IL: National Council of Teachers of English.

Gee, J. 1991. "Memory and Myth: A Perspective on Narrative." In *Developing Narrative Structure,* edited by A. McCabe and C. Peterson, 1–25. Hillside, NJ: Erlbaum.

Keebler, R. 1995. So, There Are Some Things I Don't Quite Understand . . . : An Analysis of Writing Conferences in a Culturally Diverse Second Grade Classroom. Ph.D. diss., Tufts University, Medford, MA.

Michaels, S. 1991. "The Dismantling of Narrative." In *Developing Narrative Structure,* edited by A. McCabe and C. Peterson, 303–52. Hillside, NJ: Erlbaum.

Mistry, J. 1993. "Cultural Context in the Development of Children's Narrative." In *Cognition and Culture: A Cross-Cultural Approach to Psychology,* edited by J. Altarriba, 202–20. Holland: Elsevier Science Publishers.

The number-one hesitation teachers express about undertaking a story-telling program is their own discomfort with telling stories. I strongly encourage my colleagues to overcome their stage fright. Preschoolers are extremely forgiving audiences. I stand as living proof that someone who never considered himself a storyteller can provide the adult models necessary for a successful storytelling curriculum.

Beginning tellers should seek out more experienced storytellers. These storytellers are rich sources of stories, and can serve as role models for novices. Many parts of the country now have storyteller associations, and there is a national storytelling festival held each year in Tennessee. Recordings of professional tellers are also available. My personal favorite is Jay O'Callahan. I have listened to his "The Strait of Magellan" (Artana Records, 1985) countless times.

For those just getting started telling stories, finding tales to tell can be an issue. Children love hearing about their teachers' lives, especially about their childhood. These "when I was your age" tales can be about favorite pets, family vacations, or early school experiences. Stories can also be drawn from the classics: "Three Little Pigs," "Three Billy Goats Gruff," or "Jack and the Bean Stalk." One of the nice things about stories is that you can change them around, so the Jack story can become "The Preschoolers and the Bean Stalk," with the children taking the lead role. Public libraries are stocked with folk tales. Originally told orally, these tales are easily adapted to story form.

Finally, for those searching for a story to tell, I leave you with the complete version of the Uncle Booky tale from which Beth modeled part of her story. I heard the story years before on a Folkways Record when I was searching for tales from Haiti. If the audience is unfamiliar with Uncle Booky stories, of which there are several on the Folkways recording, I begin:

> This is a story about Uncle Booky, a man from the island of Haiti. Uncle Booky lives on a farm with his wife, Madame Booky, and his nephew, Maurice. As you'll find out, Uncle Booky is very nice, but not very smart. Mme. Booky is very sensible, and Maurice is a bit of a trickster.
>
> One day Uncle Booky left his farm and walked to the market in town. When he arrived he was tired so he sat down on a bench. Across from him Uncle Booky saw an old man eating a sandwich. He took a bite of the sandwich and Uncle Booky could tell that it tasted really good. Uncle Booky went up to the man. He said, "Excuse me sir, but what kind of sandwich are you eating?" The old man didn't say anything because he was deaf and couldn't hear Uncle Booky's question. So Uncle Booky repeated his question a little louder. "Excuse me, can you tell me what kind of sandwich you're eating?" The man didn't hear and kept on eating his sandwich. Uncle Booky could tell that it was a very tasty sandwich. Uncle Booky said, "Excuse me sir, but could you please tell me what kind of sandwich you are

eating?" Just then the old man bit into a red hot pepper which was in the middle of his sandwich. "We Ah" he yelled.

"We Ah," thought Uncle Booky, "I'll have to get myself some." For the rest of the afternoon Uncle Booky searched the market for some We Ah. He went to all the stands asking, "Do you have any We Ah? Do you have any We Ah?" No one did. Dejectedly, he set off for home.

Arriving home, he saw Madame Booky. "She'll know what to do," thought Uncle Booky, and he asked hopefully, "Could you please make me a We Ah sandwich?" "If you find it, I'll cook it," Mme. Booky replied.

For the entire next week Uncle Booky roamed the island, looking for We Ah. He went to all the farms, all the markets, all the stores, searching for We Ah. But no one had any. In fact, no one had even heard of it.

Finally, Uncle Booky's nephew Maurice got tired of his uncle spending all his time looking for We Ah. He decided to play a joke on the old man. Maurice got a basket. At the bottom of the basket he put some rose branches with sharp thorns. On top of the rose branches he put some onions. On top of the onions he put some potatoes. On top of the potatoes he put some tomatoes.

Maurice brought the basket to his Uncle and announced, "Uncle Booky, I have found some We Ah for you." Well you can imagine how delighted Uncle Booky was. He grabbed the basket from Maurice, thanking him over and over.

Expectantly, Uncle Booky put his hand into the basket and pulled out a tomato. "This is not We Ah," Uncle Booky said disappointedly, "this is a tomato." Uncle Booky put his hand into the basket again, this time pulling out a potato. "This is not We Ah," Uncle Booky said emphatically, "this is a potato." Uncle Booky put his hand deeper down into the basket, and pulled out an onion. "This is not We Ah," Uncle Booky yelled indignantly, "this is an onion."

For a fourth time, Uncle Booky reached into the basket. Past the tomatoes, past the potatoes, past the onions, went his hand. Deeper and deeper, closer and closer to the rose branches. Then it happened. Reaching down, his finger was pierced by a thorn and he yelled, "WE AH!!!"

I want to thank two teacher-storytellers who inspired my program. Anne Kornblatt has stretched my thinking about children and stories for almost fifteen years, and I have stolen numerous tales from her. Vivian Paley's thoughtful, entertaining writings have launched a cadre of teacher-storytellers, of whom I am one. I also want to thank two academicians who helped further my thinking about narrative. Dr. Allysia McCabe, now at the University of

Massachusetts-Lowell, provided thoughtful encouragement when I first began looking closely at my storytelling program. Dr. Jayanthi Mistry of Tufts University was ever patient, encouraging, and insightful as I muddled through a dissertation on storytelling which was the basis for much of the above analysis.

# 7

## Sgt. Pepper and Beyond: The Beatles, the Talking Heads, and the Preschool Band

### The Preschool Band: Part 1

The Preschool Band is belting out an original composition, "Science Andrew Science," as part of a four-song concert marking their graduation from day care. The soon-to-be kindergartners sing:

> Cousin Andrew had been walking along.
> He found an extra, extra, extra science book.
> Then he wanted to see a movie camera with a flashlight.
> Then Cousin Andrew got eaten up by a shark.
> Then he went home with a Band-aid!

The song concludes with the final syllable drawn out in a fashion the children have dubbed "opera style." Smiles spread across their faces, it is clear the band has enjoyed these absurdist lyrics.

After the applause from their parents dies down, the Beatles' version of "Twist and Shout" is switched on for the group's finale. Instantaneously, the energy level changes. Pierce plays his guitar with one leg frenetically gyrating up and down. Cleo and Jerry dance their own personal versions of the Twist. Cleo's movement centers around her shoulders, which sway back and forth to the beat. Jerry, who has a look of extreme concentration, extends one leg out in front of him. With that foot pointed toward the ground, he carefully pivots on his toes. Eduardo and Lilly pound away on their makeshift drum sets. The entire group joins Paul, John, and George as they build to the famous screamed crescendo: "ah, aah, aaah, AAAAAH!" The music and the children have become one.

As I watch this graduation performance, a scene from two years prior flashes before my eyes. I see Kevin, Max, Jack, and Zack at a meeting time performing their version of "Help!" as part of a unit on the Beatles. As the tape deck blares, Max and Zack, who are Paul and George respectively, play their guitars, heads bopping side to side with the beat. Jack, who is Ringo, grins as he taps his drums. Kevin, who is John, takes the lead vocals. Standing in front of the group with a stage presence much greater than his five years, he calls out "Help, I need somebody." In the audience, my colleague Jackie Rosenbloom remarks, "It's wonderful when the curriculum and the children become one."

As the Preschool Band concludes I smile, thinking about how this group of young children came to be singing a Beatles song along with a tune about Cousin Andrew at their graduation. Somehow, in the world of preschoolers exploring music, it all makes sense.

## Why the Beatles, the Talking Heads, and the Preschool Band?

The original impetus for studying the Beatles came from Kevin and his father, Gregg. On a whim, Gregg borrowed a video of the Beatles' movie *Help!* from the public library and showed it to his family. Kevin loved the movie, and lobbied for additional Beatles films. After watching *A Hard Day's Night* Kevin had a full-fledged case of Beatlemania. At home he walked around belting out, "You've Got To Hide Your Love Away" (although he replaced "glove" for "love" as he sang). At day care he recruited his friends to "play the Beatles." Kevin proved an accomplished organizer, enticing Jack, Zack, and Max to join his band. For several days running the foursome stood in the middle of the play yard belting out, "Hey, you got to hide your glove away."

While I hadn't seriously listened to the band in a decade, watching the children play the Beatles brought back happy memories. My junior year in college I wore out a copy of *Abbey Road*. As a preteen I enjoyed the group's lively lyrics, colorful costumes, and risk-taking haircuts. For a new generation of potential fans, the band's childlike qualities—their playfulness, frivolity, boisterous energy, and penchant for colorful clothing—seemed like powerful attractions. Still, I was hesitant to make a foray into popular culture. I sensed I was violating an unwritten early childhood education taboo which prescribed more conventional topics of study. Further, as a piano lesson dropout, I was unsure about presenting a musical theme to the group. In the end, I decided to take a risk (although I hedged my bet and scheduled this initial unit for only a week). It was summertime, and after a year of serious study, a free-spirited unit was in order. The Beatles were like the circus. With Kevin as a highly persuasive advance man, I decided to bring the circus to town.

The ensuing curriculum became legendary at the day care center. When our administrator gave tours to prospective families, she was sure to mention how, "In the Preschool Room they study the Beatles." The next year parents asked about the scheduling of the unit.

While the first go-round with the Four Lads from Liverpool had been a tremendous success, I was hesitant to get the band back together. First, much of the magic of the initial study was that its impetus came from the children. No one in this next group was demonstrating a passion for the band. Second, despite the first year's success, I was aware of a serious limitation with the unit: girls felt excluded from aspects of the curriculum. The previous year, the girls enjoyed the unit's music, but were hesitant to participate in the dramatic play. Five-year-old Juliet, whose critique came from watching *A Hard Days Night*, summed up the problem, "In the Beatles, all the girls get to do is chase the boys and scream." Since playing the Beatles was the most exciting part of the unit, this was a very real concern. I also worried that children of color might experience similar feelings of exclusion.

While many teachers understand my concerns about gender, race, and curriculum, I've also had negative reactions to raising these issues. Most outrageous was one teacher's complaint, "Don't we do enough for those people already?" Generally though, unfavorable comments are milder, that I am taking multiculturalism a bit too far. I disagree. As teachers we must act in *loco parentus*. We are morally responsible *as parents* for the children in our class. Just as a mother or father would do, so we must do our best for *each* child in our care. When it comes to curriculum, the reality is that children will connect differently to topics of study. Variation is based, in part, on interests, personality, and abilities. Variation is also influenced by gender, race and ethnicity. If children don't see adults who look like them involved in a subject, they may be less inclined to study the topic. In particular, they may be unwilling to immerse themselves in the play so central to preschoolers' explorations of the world. That a topic has greater or lesser appeal to certain children is not a reason for its rejection; no topic will interest children equally. However, the issue must be on teachers' minds, and for the good of each child in the room, over the course of the year a balance among the units chosen must be reached. The second year I decided against studying the Beatles.

The next year there was again lobbying from parents for a Beatles unit. I hesitated, but in the end decided to give the unit another spin. I was happily surprised by the results, which are described below.

As part of my decision to repeat the Beatles curriculum, I brokered a compromise with myself. The compromise was that we would also study the

Talking Heads. Originally an all-White foursome, at the height of their popularity in 1982 the Talking Heads metamorphosed into a multicultural ensemble. Featuring Chris Frantz on drums, Tina Weymouth on bass guitar, Jerry Harrison and Bernie Worrell on keyboards, Alex Weir on guitar, Steve Scales playing percussion, Lynn Mabry and Ednah Holt as backing vocals, and David Byrne on guitar and lead vocals, the band is among the most diverse in rock and roll history. But the choice of the Talking Heads was much more than a nod to multiculturalism. I thought the band's unusual lyrics and offbeat style might capture the attention of preschool music fans. I noticed during the initial Beatles unit that some children were fascinated by the group's odder lyrics. Max, for example, was taken by the tune from *Abbey Road,* "You Never Give Me Your Money." He wanted to know why "the Beatles never give you their money?" and from whom cash was being withheld, finding the entire concept extremely funny. Max was not alone in relishing absurdist lyrics. Four-year-olds love nonsense. A rock group that encouraged its listeners to "stop making sense" seemed perfect for preschoolers. Finally, there was a personal factor involved. The Talking Heads are my all-time favorite band, and I looked forward to introducing them to my charges.

The Preschool Band was an outgrowth of a discussion I had with Pierce and his mother during the Talking Heads unit. Hanging out in the play yard at the end of the day, my mention of the Talking Heads caused Pierce to exclaim, "That's a funny name because heads don't talk, mouths do." He then turned to his mother and suggested, "Let's have a family band and call it the Talking Mouths." It wasn't a far leap from a family band to a class band. The idea of a class band was intriguing. Forming our own group meant the exploration of music would be taken to a different level of reality. The children would still be playing, but in that play they would be Jerry instead of John, Pierce instead of Paul. They would be imagining themselves as musicians. After we concluded our study of the Talking Heads, I asked the children if they wanted to form their own musical group. The response was enthusiastic.

The remainder of this chapter describes these four curriculum units, implemented during two separate years. The first Beatles unit was conducted with the class who participated in the first basketball unit. The second Beatles unit, the Talking Heads unit, and the Preschool Band unit made up a larger investigation of music undertaken with the group that began the year studying squirrels. Taken together, the chapter chronicles my experiments exploring music with young children and reflects on the following:

- observing children in order to understand their interests and guide their activities
- using teachers' interests and passions to determine curriculum.

Because the chapter highlights the interplay of me and the children in directing the curriculum, it vividly speaks to teaching as a dynamic process involving experimentation, reflection, and continual revision.

## Meet the Beatles

The level of Beatles' consciousness in my Preschool Room at the start of the first Beatles unit was comparable to the level of awareness in the United States before February 9, 1964. In both situations there was a small group of knowledgeable, devoted fans, while the vast majority of people were completely unaware of the band's existence. For the curriculum to be a success, those in the dark would have to be enlightened. My task was to do what Ed Sullivan did that Sunday night in 1964, and help my class meet the Beatles.

To accomplish this task I employed my standard method of introducing preschoolers to a subject: I told a story. Announcing that I was going to tell about a very famous band, fame equating with virtue for this group, I began:

> Far across the Atlantic Ocean, in Liverpool, England, there once lived a boy named John. John loved music. He loved listening to music, and he was very interested in making music. He got a guitar and practiced and practiced and practiced until he could play very well. When John was in high school he met Paul. Paul loved music as much as John, and they decided to start a band.

I then explained how George was asked to join the group, and that through practice, the boys got better and better. I continued:

> John, Paul, and George called their band the Beatles. They became well known in their city of Liverpool. After a few years they invited a man named Ringo to be the band's drummer. Soon, they became famous all over England, so famous that a man here in America heard about them. The man, Ed Sullivan, had a television show. He invited the Beatles to come play on his show, so the band traveled to New York City.

The rest, as they say, is history; a history I continued to relay to the children over the next week.

Hearing the story piqued the children's interest in the band, but what is really essential in meeting the Beatles is their music. I had great fun going through the corpus of Beatles songs, considering which would be right for a preschool audience. Eventually, I selected five tunes to feature as songs of the day: the playful "Octopus' Garden," Kevin's number-one hit, "Help!", a couple songs about friendship, "Two of Us" and "A Little Help from My Friends," and the fanciful, "You Never Give Me Your Money."

The songs of the day were introduced at meeting times. For the inaugural meeting of the unit I wrote the lyrics of "Octopus' Garden" out on a two-by-three-foot piece of paper. This "whole language" chart was adorned with symbols placed beside key words (e.g., an eight-legged figure beside each octopus). The verses appeared in blue, and the chorus in green. As I unrolled the chart I asked the children what they noticed. Maddy and Max commented on the octopi. Juliet, Miriam, and Michael noticed that the first letter of the second and third lines matched. Jack was curious about why the words were written in two colors. I explained that the green words were the chorus, which was repeated several times during the song. To illustrate the concept, I pointed to each word as Ringo sang along on the tape deck. At subsequent meetings, I introduced each song of the day with a similar chart. Questions about the choruses dominated our discussions. Beginning on the second day, instead of writing out all the words, only "chorus" appeared when the section was repeated. The children were impressed that one word could represent so many. At the end of each discussion I turned on the Beatles tape. Though optional, dancing was very popular at this point.

Taken by their music and story, all the children's interest in the Beatles quickly grew. This interest manifested itself in constant questioning about the Fab Four as the children sought to learn more about the band. When a new song was played the children wanted to know who was singing. When I showed the group the inside cover of the *Sgt. Pepper* album, I was asked, "Who's in pink?" "Who's dressed in red?" and "Who's the green guy?" When the children saw the back of the album cover they asked the question which obsessed many people in the late 1960s, "Why is the one in blue not facing the camera?"

Of particular interest was the birth order of the band. These children spent much time discussing who was the oldest, second oldest, and so on, in the class. Even though Max was only a day older than Jack, those twenty-four hours were critical in giving him the elevated status of tenth oldest preschooler. This fascination with age was now turned on the Beatles, and I was asked over and over again about the players' relative ages. For some reason though, my knowledge base was suspect. Several children insisted that, despite my answer, John was older than Ringo. Perhaps the serious guitar player struck them as more mature than the carefree drummer.

Then, on the third day of the unit, I was faced with an unexpected and unwelcome question: Who shot John? For some reason, one parent told his child John was dead. The news spread like wild-fire, and the predictable question followed: How did he die? Once that was answered, follow-up queries included, "Who shot him?" and "Why did he shoot him?" I was bombarded with questions about the tragedy, and discussions of John's death overshadowed other aspects of the curriculum. I wasn't sure what to do about the children's obsession. Fortunately, my co-teacher Cathy came up with a simple answer that satisfied the group. "Something was wrong in a person's brain, and he killed John," she explained matter of factly. With that statement, we were able to move on to other aspects of the Beatles.

Well, not completely. John's murder brought another short detour in the curriculum. Answering questions about how John died, I had editorialized a bit, concluding: "And this is one of the reasons when you pretend to shoot me, I don't like it. It reminds me of sad things like this. That's why I say I don't like guns."

For Matt's father, Bob, my commentary went too far in the "PC" slant already running rampant in his son's day care center. He did not hesitate to confront me, explaining that, "I'm very upset about you saying guns are bad. I own several guns. I enjoy hunting. I don't want my son to think his father is bad because he has guns." Bob and I had talked about guns before. He once tried to convince me to sign a petition against a bill banning assault weapons. While he was far more informed on the issue, I couldn't imagine not supporting the legislation. Bob and I were never going to see eye to eye on firearms.

But Bob did have an important point. In no way did I want to impugn the character of a father in the eyes his four-year-old son. So the next day, when Bob was doing parent help, I began meeting time by stating, "When I talked about John being shot I said how I didn't like guns. I should have also told you that adults disagree about this. For example, Bob enjoys hunting with guns. We disagree, but Bob and I are still friends."

I then asked, "What do you think about guns?" For a minute the children hemmed and hawed about the merits of weapons, seemingly unsure of their position. Jack then captured the mood of the group. He began, "My parents say guns are bad." He then quickly added, "But I like them." I smiled at Bob. Though I would have liked to, it was clear I hadn't brainwashed the children on this issue.

## Beatlemania: Part 1

It was more than idle curiosity when the children asked who was singing a particular Beatles song. These were pressing questions, figuring prominently in their dramatic play. When they were playing the Beatles, knowing who sang "Help" or "Yellow Submarine" was invaluable information, determining who would be the lead singer and who would take backup vocals. This information was in constant use. By the fourth day of the unit the children's dramatic play had been completely transformed. One theme dominated: the Beatles. Beatle-mania had struck the classroom.

Now at the start of outside time the children rushed out to the play yard. There, they quickly took up roles, shouting out, "I'm John" or "I'm Ringo." The Johns, Pauls, and Georges found shovels to be their guitars. The Ringos collected buckets and turned them over to be their drums. A series of imaginary concerts then began. This play went on for weeks, extending far past the formal conclusion of the unit.

Despite the great fun of the Beatles play, a limitation quickly became apparent: the finite number of roles in the band. Once a foursome formed, it was difficult for another child to join in, at least in a part other than that of audience. There was, after all, only one John, one Paul, one George, and one Ringo. There were hard feelings when children were excluded from groups they wished to play with because a fifth Beatle was not in the cards. Michael, who often wanted to join the Kevin, Max, Jack, and Zack foursome, was particularly hard hit by this reality.

At exploration time I tried to address this limitation. Transforming the loft into a recording studio, I gathered bongos and cymbals for a makeshift drum set, and three small guitars. I also included a computer keyboard to be used by the producer, George Martin. Martin's introduction created another attractive role. Michael, in particular, enjoyed becoming the producer, sitting behind the "mixing board," directing his friends about how loudly or softly to play. Not surprisingly, the recording studio was a very popular choice.

Even with the addition of George Martin, all the parts in the play remained male which, as previously mentioned, posed a problem. Among the girls, Juliet and Maddy were the most interested in the band, and tried out the recording studio a couple of times. Their stays did not last long. I sensed that the intensity of the boys, who were becoming band members with all their heart and soul, intimidated them from becoming more involved in an activity. The dearth of female roles was also a likely factor. At an age when gender identification comes to the fore, taking on a play role of the opposite sex might have felt taboo.

I addressed the issue of gender roles in imaginative play with a group discussion. To start, I asked, "Can a boy pretend to be a princess or a girl pretend to be a prince?" The group consensus was emphatic. Janet explained, "No! Girls have to be girls and boys have to be boys." Having received the response I expected, I challenged this thinking:

> You pretend to be lions and rhinos, but you're not wild animals, you're people. And you pretend to be mothers and fathers, but you're not grown-ups,

you're kids. So why can't a boy pretend to be a girl and a girl pretend to be a boy?

Truth be told, I didn't get a satisfactory answer here, only the sense that this group was fairly rigid in their thinking about crossing gender lines in play. I presented the position that a girl could pretend to be a boy, and encouraged girls to act out the Beatles. Still, after the unit was over, it was largely boys who continued talking about the band.

The spontaneous yard concerts and loft studio sessions were compelling, but to fully live the Beatles experience an audience was required. To provide that I brought the Beatles play to meeting time. Setting up a karaoke-style activity using the recording studio props, I called children up four at a time to be the band as "Help" played from the tape deck. While Miriam and Samantha passed, Juliet, Maddy, Janet, and Joy enthusiastically participated. All the children were very serious about their roles, and I encouraged the audience to help create the proper ambiance by waving their hands in the air and screaming. Kevin, in particular, responded to the activity. Doing a very convincing Lennon imitation, he strummed his guitar, bopped up and down to the music, and sang into an imaginary microphone. It was during his performance that Jackie Rosenbloom made her remark about the children and the curriculum becoming one.

While the formal study of the Beatles lasted only a week, its impact was felt for months. Kevin was not alone in becoming one with the curriculum. For the rest of the year children walked around humming Beatles tunes. Maddy and Jack badgered their parents to dust off old Beatles LPs, and Dan convinced his mom to purchase the CD *A Hard Day's Night*. Parents commented to me, "If I have to hear 'Help' one more time I'm going to scream." Max's family made a rule that *Sgt. Pepper's Lonely Hearts Club Band* could only be played once a day. I chuckled hearing a new generation of parents bemoaning, mostly in jest, the hold the Beatles had on their children.

## Beatlemania: Part 2

One of my favorite answering machine messages is the one that appeared on Zeeland's family's phone after the second day of his group's study of the Beatles. Before the customary instructions about leaving a message after the beeps, the tape played Zeeland singing his version of "Twist and Shout." The interpretation of the lyrics, "We're shaking up babies now, shaking the babies" was unintentionally sardonic, and his scream at the end of the recording, "ah, aah, aaah, AAAAAH!" was priceless. Beatlemania had struck again.

I was more ambitious with this second Beatles unit, allocating two weeks, and embedding it in a more general investigation of music. I began the second session by announcing that our month-long study of music would begin with a band called the Beatles. The blank looks on the children's faces caused me a bit of trepidation. Without Kevin as my advance man, would the curriculum fly? This concern was quickly put to rest.

That evening Aviva's parents dusted off their Beatles' albums, and the family danced to some of the group's greatest hits. The next day Pierce excitedly told me how he had heard the Beatles at the supermarket. Shoshana added that she had heard the Beatles on the radio. Both reports were undoubtedly aided by parents. When I began a conversation about the band at meeting Sean blurted out, "My dad knows about them." It was only the second day of study, yet the children were already enthusiastic about the unit. Parents, and the larger culture, were filling Kevin's shoes.

Successfully launched, it is fascinating how the unit played out with this second group of children. A difference I appreciated was that no one mentioned John's death. With this easygoing group, it was in character that such an intense issue was bypassed. A similarity I also appreciated was that playing the Beatles was again very popular. During outside time groups of children stood at the top of the climbing structure, pretending to give the famous rooftop rendition of "Get Back" from *Let It Be*. At exploration time, the loft recording studio was well used. This time though, gender differences did not appear in the play. Aviva and Shoshana were as enthusiastic about being Beatles as Sean and Pierce. Perhaps because no one in the group had seen *A Hard Days Night*, there was not as strict a schema for what playing the Beatles involved. In fact, the most coveted role was George Martin. The children decided he was the boss of the Beatles, having the power to determine when the playing began and ended, the volume of the music, and the assignment of solos. It was a job that girls and boys alike relished.

This group also enjoyed designing album covers. I used the cover of *Sgt. Pepper's Lonely Hearts Club Band,* with its collage of famous personalities, as a motivation for the project. To provide some context, at meeting time that day I continued telling the story of the Beatles, explaining:

> When the Beatles performed on Ed Sullivan's TV show a lot of people in the audience screamed. In fact, whenever the band played a concert most of the audience screamed, not just to applaud after a song, but when the band was playing. After a while, it seemed to the Beatles that no one was listening to the music. They all were just screaming. So the band decided to make a change. They stopped playing concerts, and only made music in the

Figure 7–1. *Jessie's illustration of the Beatles*

recording studio with the help of their friend George Martin. And they became a new group: Sgt. Pepper's Lonely Hearts Club Band.

We then listened to the title cut of the album, as well as the humorous "Good Morning, Good Morning."

The children were fascinated by the band's metamorphosis, and intrigued by the album cover. At exploration time, photos of the Beatles, the preschoolers, and of famous and not so famous people were made available. Jessie, Pierce, Eduardo, Shoshana, and Jerry were particularly interested in this material. Jerry worked on his cover for days, layering picture on top of picture, and colorizing the work with markers, inadvertently producing a very sixties style effect.

This was a group of drawers. Often children would pass up outside play to draw, and they could spend up to an hour sitting around a table with paper and markers. Soon after the unit began the Beatles became a popular subject for their sketching. The drawings ranged from the realistic to the fanciful. Jessie used the photograph on the album cover of *Something New* to produce a wonderfully accurate depiction of the group (Figure 7–1). "John With Chicken Pox" was done by Zeeland, who had just recovered from the malady (Figure 7–2).

What was most constant between the two years was the children's enthusiasm for the music. These children really liked the band, and a second group of preschoolers now walked around humming Beatles' tunes. It was time to see if they would dance to the Talking Heads.

Figure 7–2. *John with chicken pox*

## "If You Dance You'll Understand the Music Better"

The lead singer of the Talking Heads, David Byrne, once told an audience in Berlin, "If you dance you'll understand the music better." In my mind, Byrne's suggestion captures the spirit of his band, and when it comes to the Talking Heads, his advice is equally valid for English-speaking audiences as it was for that German-speaking one. There is no doubt, Talking Heads' songs are not as accessible as Beatles tunes. As a devoted fan I concede their esoteric lyrics are not for everyone. But I had a feeling they would in some way connect with a preschool perspective of the world.

At the beginning of the *Stop Making Sense* version of "Burning Down the House," if you turn the volume way up, you can hear drummer Chris Franz call out, "Anybody got a match?" To answer his question, the band launches into a classic, high energy rock 'n' roll song. It was with this question and song that I introduced the preschoolers to the Talking Heads. I told the children to listen for a surprise, and turned the tape deck up high. Pierce burst out laughing on hearing Franz's question, and then Shoshana, Aviva, Jason, and Scott couldn't help but dance when the music started.

When the song was over, I told a story about the band we were now studying:

Once there were three friends, Chris, Tina, and David, who went to art school together in Rhode Island. When they graduated the three moved to

New York City. There they started a band with their friend Jerry. Jerry played keyboards, Tina played bass guitar, Chris was the drummer, and David played guitar and sang. They called their band the Talking Heads. I'm not sure why. The band got pretty famous, and after a few years they decided to add new members. Bernie came on as a keyboard player. Steve played percussion instruments like the tambourine. Alex played guitar, and Lynn and Ednah sang.

I then explained how this expanded version of the Talking Heads made a legendary concert tour called "Stop Making Sense," and how I had seen a performance when I was just out of college.

It wasn't until he saw the movie *Stop Making Sense* that my Swiss friend Walter became a Talking Head fan. Until then, he regarded this band with a strange name as a weird kind of American cult phenomenon. Seeing a live performance, with its humorous antics and contagious energy, forever changed Walter's opinion. I thought the concert video might have similar effect on the children. Seeing the movie would also provide my class with visual images of musicians at work, images I thought would inspire dramatic play.

That afternoon my class watched two cuts from the *Stop Making Sense* video: "Cross-Eyed and Painless" and "Once in a Lifetime." Jason, Aviva, and Scott responded immediately to the film, dancing around to the music. Shoshana and Eduardo at first didn't know what to make of the concert, and stared at the screen. Later, they joined the dancing. Pierce watched intently, playing air guitar throughout. Afterward we chatted about the video, which received very favorable reviews. I asked the children what they noticed about the concert. Pierce mentioned how, "Alex and David were hugging" while playing guitars. Lilly said she liked the drumming. Aviva and Shoshana talked about Lynn and Ednah's long hair flying around as they danced. Jerry remembered how, "David threw his hat" into the audience, and Scott recalled how David screamed, "like the Beatles." I knew the video had made a strong impression when, after the screening, several children drew pictures of the band (Figure 7–3).

Having seen the band in action, I now wanted to provide the children opportunities to play the Talking Heads. With a keyboard, a tambourine, and an adult sports jacket (to be David Byrne's "big suit") added to the drums and guitars, the loft "recording studio" opened the next day at exploration time. Earlier that day, I mentioned how drummer Chris and bassist Tina had a baby. This bit of information, and the fact that the loft was directly above the house area, led to an unexpected and delightful dramatic play scenario best described as "the Talking Heads go domestic."

Figure 7–3. *Child's illustration of the Talking Heads*

My favorite scene from this play involved Aviva and Shoshana. Shoshana had been up in the loft, drumming away as Scott, Eduardo, and Jerry sang "Burning Down the House" at the top of their lungs. The song completed, Aviva left the loft. Entering the house, she called to Shoshana, who was holding a doll:

*Aviva:* Hi Tina!

*Shoshana:* Hi Chris!

*Aviva:* How's the baby?

*Shoshana:* Hungry.

Shoshana then handed Aviva the doll, and went up to the loft to make music. Aviva remained in the house, dancing around with the doll on her shoulder as she prepared dinner for the rest of the band. In a few minutes the whole ensemble came down from the loft and ate an imaginary feast of ice cream, fish, and peanut butter and jelly sandwiches. Of course, everyone asked after the baby.

With music in the air, both the Beatles and Talking Heads units afforded opportunities to discuss composition; who wrote particular songs, where the ideas for songs came from, the synthesis of words and lyrics to form a song, and how music and words were notated. Song writing was a natural exploration

Figure 7–4. *Children composing music*

time activity. Borrowing an idea from a former student teacher, Sarah Marcus, I showed the group sheet music. After discussing the symbols on the score, children were invited to compose their own songs. With an adult available to write down words, the young musicians were provided paper with oversized, empty staffs. Sheets with free-form treble clefs, random quarter notes, and fanciful lyrics resulted. For example, Eduardo wrote an environmental piece entitled "Charles River" that went "No garbage. No garbage. No more. The end." Zeeland was poetic, entitling his song, "Come with Me Across the Space of Time." Alexandra's "The Scream" was simply a yell, while Shoshana's ballad, "I Love Mommy," reflected the topic closest to a preschooler's heart.

Scott and Jessie took their compositions very seriously. After filling the staff paper with a series of random notes, they brought their songs up to the loft. There they carefully studied the notations as they strummed guitars, playing their music. With music of their own, the children were ready to form their own band.

## The Preschool Band: Part 2

In seventh grade my friend Ari and I decided to form a rock band. Ari was the bass player. Our friend David played bongos. Too shy to appear on stage, I volunteered to be the manager. I can't remember if the group ever rehearsed, and I know it never performed a concert. The group did, after weeks of deliberation, settle one critical issue. We picked a name for our band: Sheridan Road.

The first order of business as our investigation of music turned from the Beatles and the Talking Heads to the class band was clear: naming the group. Just as it did for Ari and myself, a name would provide an identity. It would make the endeavor seem real. Brainstorming produced some egocentric ideas (the Scott Band, the Shoshanas), along with some surprisingly savvy suggestions (DASH, the Carpet Squares, and my favorite, Science Movie Camera). A democratic classroom, the selection process was done by vote. Ultimately, a more conventional name, the Preschool Band, was chosen.

So named, the children were enthusiastic about this undertaking. Still, for the Preschool Band to go further than Sheridan Road did, I needed to be a better manager than I was back in seventh grade. While the children had an emerging sense of band from studying the Beatles and Talking Heads, a good deal of support and guidance was needed for the group to be more than just a name.

My first move as the Preschool Band's manager was to book a concert date. I arranged with Maggie Ashton, the afternoon Stomper Room (three-year-old) teacher, to have her class visit the following week. I featured the upcoming gig on our class calendar. Having a performance scheduled brought a sense of purpose to our endeavor.

A concert date booked, the band needed some material. The need led to a second stab at composing. This time the children produced more expansive lyrics. "Science Andrew Science," the song sung at graduation, came from this activity. Written by Sean about his two obsessions, science and his teenaged cousin, I added a simple tune to the lyrics to complete a song I suspect David Byrne would appreciate. The other children had heard all about Cousin Andrew; he was part of classroom lore. There was no doubt, "Science Andrew Science" was going to be part of the band's premier performance.

We spent the next two days filling out the play list. After a brainstorming session and a series of votes, the rock 'n' roll version of "ABC" and "Twist and Shout" were added. Then, based on children's preferences, I assigned instruments. Lilly and Eduardo were the two drummers. Jerry, Pierce, and Aviva played guitar. Keesha and Scott were on tambourine. We spent the next few meeting times rehearsing for the big day. At exploration time, the children continued to write songs, play up in the recording studio, and design album covers, now for the Preschool Band.

On the appointed day the Stompers filed in and took their seats. On stage stood the Preschoolers, holding their instruments. I introduced the group, and they launched into the "ABCs." The Stompers sat in silence, staring in awe at these "big kids." At the time I couldn't read their reactions, but learned later that the performance made a big impression. Two months later, one of the first things these children did after their transition to the Preschool Room was stand in the middle of the play yard holding long-handled shovels as guitars and belt out the "ABCs."

As for the band members, it was clear they were having fun. With big smiles on their faces they bopped around the stage. They clearly relished screaming along to "Twist and Shout." After The Stompers departed they congratulated each other. Like Jerry Harrison and Alex Weir in the *Stop Making Sense* video, Pierce and Jerry hugged. The Preschoolers had done a wonderful job together, and clearly felt good about themselves for doing so.

The concert was the capstone experience in our investigation of music. That evening I said good-bye to the Preschoolers, and left on a six-week summer vacation. I returned in mid-August, with two weeks remaining in the preschool year. Before I went on vacation, I showed the group a calendar of the summer, telling them, "There are lots and lots of days left before you leave for kindergarten. If you want to talk about it now we can. We'll talk about graduating and going to your new school later. But for now, it's still a while away, and it's too soon to worry about it." On my return it was time to worry about it, or at least to talk about it. I took out the calendar and pointed out the passage of time, noting the ten days until "the last day." Quoting Robert McCloskey's *Time of Wonder* (New York: Viking, 1957) I explained, "Kids are probably feeling a little bit sad about the place they are leaving, a little bit glad about the place they are going." When Pierce asked what we were going to be studying I replied, "Graduation."

Graduation was scheduled for Friday, August 28, at 5:00 P.M. The fifteen-minute ceremony involved rituals designed to bring closure to the children and their families leaving a day care center that some had attended since infancy. The year of the first Beatles unit, graduation ended with "The Long and Winding Road" playing as a banner signed by the children was raised. That year there wasn't a dry eye in the audience.

I had a few preconceived notions about the form of this next graduation. Repeating the banner raising was a must, though this year "Nkosi Sikelel Afrika," the South African national anthem, would play. To involve the children in planning, I invited their suggestions. Zeeland requested "a store-bought cake." Sean wanted brownies. Jerry hoped for pirate costumes. At the end of the brainstorming I offered my suggestion: reuniting the Preschool Band.

The idea met with an enthusiastic and kinesthetic reaction. Along with the cheers, Eduardo, Pierce, and Shoshana began playing air guitar. I took this reaction as an endorsement that the band was to be part of the ceremony.

Which is how the preschoolers came to be singing about Cousin Andrew at their graduation.

## "Why Don't You Teach Them Real Music?"

When I first announced we were going to study the Beatles, Fred's mother, a classical pianist, snapped, "Why don't you teach them real music?" Not one for quick rejoinders, I shrugged off the comment. That night I wished I'd retorted, "the Beatles are *real* music," citing Louis Armstrong's criteria for evaluating music: "If it sounds good, it is good." At the time I was also unsure as to how the curriculum would proceed. Now, with the experience of several units behind me, I would also reply that studying certain pop bands can provide a very accessible way for children to explore the world of music.

The heightened musical awareness of my students that emerged from studying the Beatles, the Talking Heads, and the Preschool Band was impressive. Superficially, the children's vocabularies expanded to include *lyrics, chorus, verses, instrumentals,* and *solos.* More substantially, the way the children listened to music changed. They became more careful, informed listeners. They now paid attention to the instruments used, focusing on the harmonica in "Love Me Do" and the piano introduction to "You Never Give Me Your Money." They noticed vocal qualities, distinguishing between John's rougher and Paul's smoother voice. They enjoyed musical jokes like the false ending of "Hello Good-bye" where Michael felt, "They try to fool you." During the second year, they also developed a sense of bandness, comparing and contrasting the Beatles and Talking Heads, and asking about other musical groups.

Seeing this happen changed Fred's mother's opinion of the Beatles unit. Others might still disapprove of studying something as lowbrow as pop music. On a fundamental level, my view of education differs from these critics. For some, education involves furnishing children's minds with skills and knowledge. Knowledge involves the key achievements of our culture, and in music, that knowledge should be the classics: Beethoven, Bach, Mozart. I agree that skills and knowledge are very good things (and enjoy listening to classical music). But I see education involving more than cognition, more than filling up children's minds. Educational experiences also intentionally or unintentionally influence children's dispositions to learn. A central part of my job is building on children's natural curiosity about the world, so they come to see themselves as learners. That is why I put so much stock in children's enthusiasm for a unit of study. That is why I use dramatic play as a criteria for evaluating a unit's success. That is why I've adopted Eleanor Duckworth's (1987) credo, that the cornerstone of education is helping children have wonderful ideas, *and helping them feel good about having them.* That is why I introduced these chapters by talking about love.

I consider these investigations of music successful because they helped children's feelings for music grow. They heard new music, thought about it in new ways, and began to see themselves, through play, as musicians. A comment Max made to his mother several months after our study illustrates the lasting impact of the music curriculum. Driving home from day care he confided to her, "Jack, Kevin, Zack, and I have been practicing a lot. When we grow up we're going to be the Beatles. When we have a concert, I'll call you up."

## Resources

The music of the Beatles changed significantly over time. Some fans prefer the early, basic rock 'n' roll songs. Others enjoy the more expansive, complex later works. My opinion is the group produced great music throughout their tenure together. If forced to choose one album to take to a desert island, I'd pick either *Sgt. Pepper's Lonely Hearts Club Band* or *Abbey Road.* All the band's music is readily available on both original albums and greatest hit anthologies at local record shops.

While CDs may represent a technological advance over LPs, cover art has suffered in the transition to the smaller format. If you haven't saved your college record collection, or are too young to have one, used record stores provide an inexpensive way to obtain your copy of *Sgt. Pepper's Lonely Hearts Club Band.*

A bookcase could be filled with the volumes written about the Beatles. My friend Ari recommends *The Beatles: The Biography* by Hunter Davies (New York: Norton, 1996) as a good way to become acquainted with Beatles lore. *The Beatles Anthology,* a video that originally aired over four nights on television, is also a very enjoyable introduction (or reintroduction) to the Fab Four. Copies are available at video and music stores.

The Talking Heads are far less well known than the Beatles. Still, a good record store should have a fair number of Talking Heads CDs. The best cuts off the band's first five releases, *Talking Heads '77* (Sire, 1977), *More Songs About Buildings and Food* (Sire, 1978), *Fear of Music* (Sire, 1979), *Remain in Light* (Sire, 1980), and *Speaking in Tongues* (Sire, 1983) are included on the sound track of their 1984 film *Stop Making Sense.* The live versions of "Once in a Life Time" and "Take Me to the River" run longer than their studio counterparts, and in my opinion, have more energy. "Road to Nowhere" off the *Little Creatures* CD (Sire, 1985) is a great dance tune. Lead singer David Byrne's solo endeavor *The Catherine Wheel* (Sire, 1991), the score to a dance performance by Twyla Tharp, is music that inspires children to think of many ways to move.

Clearly, there are other musicians worthy of study. Every year my class celebrates Mozart's birthday (January 27). At meeting that day I tell my students a bit of the composer's biography, and have them close their eyes to enjoy pianist Alicia DeLoroca's performance of the *Rondo in D Major*. The music inspires vivid imagery. However, I am not well enough versed in Mozart's work to lead an entire unit on the study of the composer.

A musician I am more familiar with, and am considering introducing to my class, is Paul Simon. Simon has a vast and varied song book, ranging from his youthful collaborations with Art Garfunkel (*Bridge over Troubled Water,* 1970) to his smash hit *Graceland* (Warner, 1986) to his more recent work for the stage *Cape Man* (Warner, 1997). Simon's beautiful ballads, upbeat dance tunes, and often comical lyrics make him an attractive candidate for study. At the very least, his tune "Cars Are Cars (All over the World)" is a must for any unit on transportation.

I want to thank Ari Mintz for giving me the six-record set *The Beatles: Alpha-Omega* for my Bar Mitzvah. It was a wonderful introduction to the band. More recently, Ari served as fact checker for this essay, though I take full responsibility for any remaining errors in Beatles legend and lore.

# *Thinking* Big
## Some Final Thoughts

**M**y wife affectionately says that I'm good at developing early childhood curriculum because, deep down inside, I'm four years old. She is right as usual. One of my strengths as a teacher is that I can draw upon my "inner child" to think, and feel, like a preschooler.

In this regard, I'm like Josh Baskin, a character Tom Hanks portrayed in one of his early films, *Big*. Josh is a typical preadolescent from suburban New Jersey. One night, after encountering Zolitor, a mysterious fortune-telling machine, Josh's body—but not his mind—is magically transformed into adulthood. After a series of madcap adventures, Josh lands a job in Manhattan as a toy developer. The newly minted grown-up instantly becomes a star of the profession, running rings around doubting experts because he is in touch with how children think.

Creating compelling early childhood curriculum requires "thinking *Big*" in the Josh Baskin sense. While I don't always succeed in such thinking, the success I have stems from bringing a sense of wonder to the world, understanding the role of story and play in curriculum, maintaining spontaneity in teaching, and, ultimately, having faith in children.

Zen philosophers refer to what I call a sense of wonder about the world as "child's mind." Thinking *Big* involves achieving child's mind, looking at the world afresh and full of wonder—in short, from a child's perspective. My thirty-something mind is too jaded and preoccupied to achieve this with any regularity, but every once in a while something will hit me. I'll know "the kids will really love this." The "this" might be a sunset, the height of Manute Bol, or the Beatles costumes on the cover of *Sgt. Pepper's Lonely Hearts Club Band*. Being open to an event or material or place that might interest preschoolers is part of creating compelling curriculum.

Understanding the role of story and play in curriculum again necessitates relating to the world from a child's perspective. Young children love stories. The surest way to catch a preschooler's attention is to begin a story. Author Eudora Welty, remembering her own childhood, describes it perfectly:

Long before I wrote stories, I listened for stories. Listening *for* them is something more acute than listening *to* them. I suppose it's an early form of participation in what goes on. Listening children know stories are *there*. When their elders sit and begin, children are just waiting and hoping for one to come out, like a mouse from its hole. (1984, 14)

As for play, young children live much of their lives in the realm of fantasy. For preschoolers, half-eaten crackers become giraffes and guns. Walks to the park can be trips to the moon. Bill Watterson, the creator of *Calvin and Hobbes,* hit the mark with his depiction of Calvin, a youngster who effortlessly slips in and out of the make-believe world. Thinking *Big* involves sensing where stories and play can enhance study. It means realizing that an observatory will enrich the study of astronomy, that hearing about Rebecca Lobo will interest children in basketball, and accepting an invitation from an imaginary friend named Ashraf will propel children's exploration of South Africa.

Spontaneity is a hallmark of childhood. Unlike the methodical, plodding adults they will develop into, children are unable to behave in a linear, planful manner. They shift their focus of attention with sometimes dizzying speed. At play, preschoolers change from knights into dinosaurs in the blink of an eye. In conversations, talk about birthdays evolve into discussions of grandmothers without warning. While part of a teacher's job is to rein in children's channel surfing, a degree of classroom spontaneity is also a hallmark of good teaching. For teachers, spontaneity involves following ideas that appear in class. It means abandoning plans, as David Hawkins puts it, to uncover rather than cover the curriculum. A commitment to spontaneity is the reason my plan book is only half filled at the beginning of the week, and why my lesson plans are never faithfully followed. I can't know on Monday what compelling curriculum on Friday will involve until I see my class' reaction to a subject. I can't plan follow-up activities until I see what interests children in the initial activities. Spontaneity created *The Crazy Squirrel Book,* the children's encounter with asteroids in the story of their travels through the solar system, and the Preschool Band. Thinking *Big* in this vein is like jazz. You know some of the notes you'll improvise, taking inspiration from the members of your band. Working with children's spontaneous impulses is essential in the search for compelling curriculum.

Of course, there is more to creating compelling curriculum than thinking like a preschooler, just as there is more to designing toys than thinking like a child. At the end of *Big,* Josh Baskin flees Manhattan, desperately trying to return to his former life. In mind, Josh is still a child, not ready for the adult world. Designing toys and creating compelling early childhood curriculum also necessitates thinking big in an adult sense.

I use adult here in its most positive connotation, involving a measure of maturity, perspective, and wisdom. As guardians of the next generation, we are preparing children to be members of society and ideally, to transform society for the better. Schooling is far more than entertainment, and creating compelling curriculum is more than identifying activities that children will like. Teachers must look beyond the classroom and understand the larger context in which their work falls; they must reflect and think critically about their practice.

Much more can be said about thinking big in an adult sense, but most of it should be self-evident. I stress the child's sense of thinking *Big* here because I've become aware that a surprising number of adults have stopped thinking *Big*. Among this group are parents, program administrators, and even fellow teachers. The unfortunate truth is that some people just won't get it when your class studies squirrels, South Africa, or the Beatles.

I can undertake such topics in my class, risking raised eyebrows and failure (not all curriculum works out), because I have faith in my students; faith in their curiosity, faith in their intelligence, and faith in our relationships. Such faith in who (or what) you are working with is embodied in the person of Joe Patroni, a character in the seventies disaster film *Airport*. In the film George Kennedy plays Patroni, a gruff, cigar-smoking aviation mechanic who loves airplanes. Because of his renowned expertise, Patroni is given the urgent task of clearing a runway so a disabled airliner, piloted by Dean Martin, can land safely in the midst of a raging blizzard. In one of the classic scenes of American cinema, Kennedy is in the cockpit of a Boeing 707, which is stuck in the snow, blocking the runway. His young sidekick gasps in disbelief as Kennedy tries to maneuver the stranded plane through a snow bank. As the engines roar and the plane shakes, Kennedy skillfully guides the plane safely off the landing strip. The stunned sidekick gasps, "The instruction book said that was impossible." Kennedy calmly responds, "That's the nice thing about the 707, it can do everything but read."

I've heard similar comments about preschoolers, that they can't or shouldn't study such abstract topics as astronomy and South Africa, or that they are too young to look inside a squirrel. To my delight, I have found that preschoolers, not unlike the Boeing 707, can do just about everything but read. At least most can't read, and the few who can haven't read about what they can't do. Preschoolers think, create, love, and constantly surprise me. Together, we discover the world.

# References

Herrigel, E. 1971. *Zen in the Art of Archery.* Translated by R. Hull. New York: Vintage Books.

Watterson, B. 1987. *Calvin and Hobbes.* Kansas City, MO: Andrews and McMeel.

Welty, E. 1984. *One Writer's Beginning.* Cambridge, MA: Harvard University Press.

# Further Readings

M ost likely, readers have heard the echoes of other books in the pages above. Without question, my teaching has been influenced by some insightful writers whose ideas have been incorporated into this volume. The suggested readings that follow make up a personal bibliography, listing some vital resources that have helped me in crafting compelling curriculum.

I first read several of the essays that are included in Eleanor Duckworth's *The Having of Wonderful Ideas* during my teacher-training program at Wheelock College. The book is the gold standard for writings about what is alternatively called developmental, constructivist, and/or progressive education. The essays' themes are far-ranging, including how teachers can engage children with phenomena, the importance of allowing for children's unexpected ideas when implementing lessons, and ways to meaningfully evaluate curriculum. Duckworth's credo that "the essence of pedagogy is to give learners the occasion to have wonderful ideas, and to let them feel good about themselves for having them" is an essential antidote for teachers struggling against the misguided position that even our youngest children must be force-fed "basic skills."

It was at Wheelock that I also read, and met, the distinguished husband-and-wife team of David and Frances Hawkins. A philosopher by training, David Hawkins writes about the theoretical underpinnings which guide effective pedagogy. His work, *The Informed Vision,* sets out some powerful ideas about curriculum and the nature of student-teacher relationships. Best described as a teacher's teacher, Frances Hawkins writes passionately about how really smart young children are. Her book, *The Logic of Action,* includes many compelling physical science activities along with explanations about how instruction can emerge from a deep respect for children. The capstone experience of my time at Wheelock was the Hawkinses' visit to my student-teaching seminar. Meeting David and Frances inspired me to realize that I had joined a teaching lineage, a pedagogical tradition that values children and sets out ways adults can support their development. David and Frances are the mentors of my most important instructor at Wheelock, Karen Worth. The Hawkinses speak of influential teachers in their lives and have the writings of David's mother's kindergarten teacher (circa 1875) on their bookshelf. They also refer to colleagues around the country and across the globe. Since then I have often taken comfort in knowing my work in the classroom is part of something bigger, part of a movement that stretches back in time and around the world.

The sense of the connectedness that history can inspire is the reason I recommend reading John Dewey. Dewey is the grandfather of developmental or constructivist education. Reading Dewey, one realizes that many of the "new" trends in education are actually a century old. It is thus not a lack of ideas that mitigates against good instruction. Each generation of teachers must fight the good fight to create classrooms and schools that best serve children. Dewey's *Democracy and Education* broadly addresses the issue of moral education, setting out how teachers can prepare our charges to be active citizens.

After graduating from Wheelock I continued reading to keep my teaching mind well exercised. Coming across Vivian Paley's (1979) *White Teacher*, I encountered a writer engaging to fellow educators in an intelligent, stimulating manner. Reading the corpus of Paley's work (*Wally's Stories, Mollie Is Three, You Can't Say You Can't Play*) has fundamentally changed how I teach. I have introduced a storytelling program, focused more on children's emotional lives, and each year consciously strive to create a classroom community among my students. Most important, I have tried to adopt Paley's reflection, experimentation, and continual revision in my pedagogy.

After teaching for several years, I returned to academia, enrolling in a Ph.D. program at Tufts University's Eliot-Pearson Department of Child Study. At Tufts I was introduced to the writings of Soviet psychologist Lev Vygotsky. Vygotsky has been called the Mozart of developmental psychology, a gifted, prolific theorist who died young. Reading his *Mind in Society* (1978) was a challenging experience. The volume describes how cognitive development is inherently social, and how adults can guide and stretch children's thinking. Since reading Vygotsky I have been working on implementing his insights in a manner respectful of my students' emotional needs.

A better understanding of children's emotional needs is gained from Erik Erikson's *Childhood and Society* (1950). The chapter on "The Eight Ages of Man" presents a dynamic theory of life-span development. Brimming with truths about young children, the work is invaluable when making curricular decisions. Admittedly, Erikson's writing is dense. While it bears reading, and rereading, a more accessible introduction to Erikson's ideas is the animated film *Everyone Rides the Carousel.* A blue-ribbon winner at the American Film Festival, the movie poignantly outlines the psychological struggles humanity faces from infancy to old age.

We live in a world with a tragic legacy of discrimination. While there have been important strides in recent decades, equality is still more a dream than a reality. Lisa Delpit's *Other People's Children* raises an issue all teachers must confront: how culture should influence instruction. Questions of race, culture, and gender must be kept in mind as we teach. Delpit's provocative essays will shake the compliancy about these issues out of anyone who reads them, providing important ideas about how to help children from traditionally disenfranchised backgrounds learn the skills of the mainstream *and* maintain their own identities.

Finally, I want to mention a book not from education or the allied fields of anthropology, psychology, or economics. Donald Murray's (1996) *Crafting a Life* is a book about writing. My reading of Murray coincided with starting work on this volume; his humorous, thoughtful stories helped me see myself as an author. I believe I have become a better teacher over the last few years because writing these pages has helped me look more closely at my own practice. While you certainly don't have to write a book to be a good teacher, the self-analysis involved in writing (even for an audience of one, as in a journal) is invaluable.

# References

Delpit, L. 1995. *Other People's Children: Cultural Conflict in the Classroom.* New York: Free Press.

Dewey, J. 1968. *Democracy and Education: An Introduction to the Philosophy of Education.* New York: Free Press.

Duckworth, E. 1987. *"The Having of Wonderful Ideas" and Other Essays on Teaching and Learning.* New York: Teachers College Press.

Erikson, E. 1950. *Childhood and Society.* New York: Norton.

Hawkins, D. 1974. *The Informed Vision: Essays on Learning and Human Nature.* New York: Agathon.

Hawkins, F. 1969. *The Logic of Action: Young Children at Work.* Boulder: Colorado Associated University Press.

Murray, D. 1996. *Crafting a Life in Essay, Story, Poem.* Portsmouth, NH: Boynton/Cook.

Paley, V. 1979. *White Teacher.* Cambridge, MA: Harvard University Press.

———. 1981. *Wally's Stories.* Cambridge, MA: Harvard University Press.

———. 1986. *Mollie Is Three: Growing Up in School.* Chicago: University of Chicago Press.

———. 1992. *You Can't Say You Can't Play.* Cambridge, MA: Harvard University Press.

Vygotsky, L. 1978. *Mind in Society: The Development of Higher Psychological Processes.* Cambridge, MA: Harvard University Press.